GOOD NEWS IN
CORINTHIANS I & II

*Paul's First and
Second Letters to the Corinthians
in Today's English Version*

Introduced by
WILLIAM NEIL

Collins
FONTANA BOOKS
in co-operation with The Bible Reading Fellowship

First published in Fontana Books 1977
© William Neil 1977

Today's English Version of
Paul's First and Second Letters to the Corinthians
© American Bible Society, New York, 1966, 1971

Made and printed in Great Britain by
William Collins Sons & Co. Ltd, Glasgow

CONTENTS

PREFACE

The four gospels – Matthew, Mark, Luke and John –
tell us more or less all we know of the life and teaching
of Jesus. The epistles – mainly written by St Paul –
carry the story forward and show us how the impact of
Jesus worked out in the earliest stages of the Church that
he founded. No other New Testament letters give us a
clearer picture of the day-to-day problems that faced
these scattered Christian communities around the
Mediterranean than the letters which Paul wrote to
Corinth. Here we find the apostle facing up to the questions which perplexed the young congregations and gave
Paul cause for both anxiety and joy. First Corinthians
opens the door on questions that are still of vital concern
to churches everywhere. How should Christians live in
a pagan world? Is Christian behaviour possible amid the
specious attractions of city life?

Far from finding a glamorous picture of these early
Christians as passionately devoted to Christ and his
cause, we read of quarrels and factions, sexual mal-
practice and drunken debauches. In the midst of all
this Paul retains his faith in God and his concern for his
wayward flock. Moreover he has important things to
say about what we now call Pentecostalism and gives us
the earliest account of Christ's resurrection. But the gem
of the letter is his inspired hymn in praise of Christian
love in chapter 13. In Second Corinthians he tells of
many of his adventures and misadventures which we
do not hear of elsewhere, including his spiritual experiences. All in all, the letters to Corinth are an invaluable
part of the New Testament and a treasure-house of
Christian insights. For those who wish to go more
deeply into the text of *1* and *2 Corinthians* the commentaries of C. K. Barrett will be found most helpful.

WILLIAM NEIL

Nottingham
September 1976

PAUL'S FIRST LETTER
TO THE CORINTHIANS

We might be expected to know that the Corinthians
were natives of Corinth and that Corinth is in Greece,
and even that we get our word 'currants' from Corinth
where they originally came from. But what had St Paul
to do with the place, and why did he write four letters
to the Christians in Corinth, not just two as the New
Testament seems to imply? Paul was an inveterate
traveller, tireless in his missionary work throughout
the whole of the Near East and reaching into what we
now call Europe as far as Rome. But in addition to his
travels, which involved preaching and teaching, he was
an assiduous letter writer – both to individuals and to
small groups of Christians whom he had visited or hoped
to visit. This was one of the secrets of his outstanding
success as a missionary.

There was no regular postal service in the civilized
world in Paul's day, except for official military or diplo-
matic communication. Letters had to be entrusted to
friends or strangers who happened to be going by sea or
land to the required destination. It is thus not surprising
that many of Paul's letters were lost in transit. But we
have enough of them which were eventually collected
and found a place in the New Testament to enable us to
see the kind of things Paul was concerned with – problems
in the various churches on which he had been asked for
his advice, disputes which he had been invited to settle,
rebukes which as a father in God he felt he must admin-
ister, messages of encouragement and congratulation,
sharp words or kindly words as the occasion demanded.
They are all to be found here in his letters to the church
at Corinth which provide a miniature mirror of the great
apostle's mind, help us to know him as he was, and
explain his power to move and inspire a whole range of
men and women, young and old, and to communicate
to them some of his own devotion to the service of
Christ.

If we turn for a moment to the book of *Acts* (15:36–18:22) we can read there of Paul's second missionary journey, which was to take him to Corinth for the first time. He and his companions had come through Asia Minor visiting some of the Christian communities he had founded on a previous tour. Then, crossing the Aegean, he set foot in Europe for the first time and began forming Christian groups there too, such as those at Philippi and Thessalonica, to which he afterwards wrote the letters which are now part of the New Testament.

His visit to Athens was the least successful from a missionary point of view. It was the home of poets and philosophers and the most cultured city in the ancient world. Paul did his best to meet the Athenians on their own ground, quoting Greek poetry and arguing in a way which he thought would be acceptable to Greek minds. But he made little impression and very few converts and left Athens with his spirits at low ebb. It seems that he was also far from well at the time, so when he reached Corinth, his next port of call, the outlook was not promising. To go from Athens to Corinth was like going from Cambridge to Birmingham. Athens was a provincial university town, Corinth was a commercial metropolis, a seaport of half a million about fifty miles from Athens, with a large Jewish colony, a cosmopolitan population and a reputation for profligacy and sexual licence which was proverbial in the ancient world. In popular jargon to 'corinthianize' meant to fornicate.

Paul arrived in Corinth about AD50 and stayed there for eighteen months before returning to his headquarters at Antioch in Syria. He found work at his trade of tentmaking with a Jewish couple – Aquila and Priscilla – and to begin with, made his home with them. He started his missionary campaign in the Jewish synagogue, but opposition was so great that he publicly announced his intention of leaving the Jews to their own devices and concentrating on a mission to the Gentiles. This he did with considerable success, and many were converted to the Christian faith.

After his return to Antioch, Paul's next venture was

to Ephesus in Asia Minor, which he made the centre of a wide-ranging missionary enterprise for himself and his associates for about three years. It was while he was deeply involved in this that bad news came to him from Corinth. Remember that Corinth was notorious as the moral cesspool of Greece, and that it was from this background that many of Paul's converts came. He refers to them politely as, on the whole, not 'wise or powerful or of high social status' (*1 Cor.* 1:26), but he later goes further and suggests that some of them came from the dregs of society (*1 Cor.* 6:9–11). It is not surprising therefore that after Paul's departure some of the Corinthian church members fell back into their old ways. Particularly, the sex-laden atmosphere of the pagan temples was hard to resist.

Apparently Paul wrote a strong letter to Corinth warning the Christians there of the danger of associating with bad characters claiming to be Christians. This first letter to Corinth has been lost but Paul refers to it in *1 Corinthians* 5:9. He got a letter back which he mentions in *1 Corinthians* 7:1. In this letter a number of questions were asked which required an answer – practical problems on which the apostle's advice was sought. Not only that, but further bad reports had come to Paul which needed firm handling. Accordingly, to answer the questions that had been put to him by the Corinthian Christians and to leave them in no doubt about his views on what was meant by Christian behaviour, he wrote a letter which is known to us in the New Testament as the First Letter to the Corinthians. This was in AD54.

1:1-9 Blessings in Christ
Paul begins his letter in the usual fashion of the time with some words of greeting. But there is a difference. Paul never wastes words. As we shall see later, his authority is being called in question. 'What right has this man to tell us what to do?' So in his first few words he puts the record straight; he is writing not as a casual busybody, but as one who was commissioned by God to be an 'apostle', someone who is 'sent out' (which is what the word 'apostle' means) to tell the good news about

Christ, and what greater authority could a man have? Paul's encounter with the risen Christ on the road to Damascus (*Acts* 26:12–18) had not only changed the whole course of his life, but had given him an invincible assurance that he had been called to a unique vocation.

In writing this letter Paul associates with himself one of his fellow-workers, Sosthenes. Nothing is known about this man unless he is perhaps the same person who is mentioned in *Acts* 18:17 as the leader of the synagogue at Corinth, who was beaten up in front of the Roman governor, and who may subsequently have been converted. Paul then goes on to give thanks to God for his grace in calling the members of the Corinthian church into the fellowship of God's people and, in passing, refers to the belief which dominated the life of the early Church that Christ would shortly return and be seen in all his glory. This will be the 'Day of our Lord Jesus Christ' when he comes to judge the world.

1:10-17 Divisions in the Church

Paul believed passionately in the unity of the Church, which is the body of Christ. It was difficult enough to make people at Corinth feel that they belonged to the same fellowship as Christians in Thessalonica and Philippi, to say nothing of Antioch and Jerusalem. But it was appalling to hear that there were actually divisions within a single congregation, with groups claiming to belong to different parties, swearing allegiance to one or other of the missionary leaders. This was what had been reported to Paul at Ephesus by some members of the Corinthian congregation who had brought the bad news. One of these groups claimed to be loyal to Paul himself, the founder of their church. Another faction preferred the eloquent preacher Apollos who had spent some time in Corinth and made a deep impression (*Acts* 18:24–28). Others again claimed to be supporters of Peter, although there is no evidence that Peter ever came to Corinth. Probably they were Jewish Christians who resented Paul's pre-eminence over the chief of the Twelve. The oddest group consisted of some who alleged that they were pledged to Christ alone. This looks as if they were priding themselves on having a special relationship to Christ and being a cut above the rest.

But Paul will have none of this. They are behaving as if Christ could be divided up, each group getting a share. All the church leaders are subordinate to Christ. He alone died for all and it is in his name alone that all must be baptized. Paul knows his place in the Church. He recalls now by name the handful of people he has himself baptized. There is thus no danger of his thinking of himself as leader of a faction. His vocation is to be a preacher of the Good News, and that without any oratorical devices, which might deflect the listeners' thoughts from the central message of the preacher which must be Christ's death on a cross.

1:18-31 Christ the Power and the Wisdom of God

Perhaps it was his failure in Athens to win over the intellectuals that decided Paul that his message must now be the stark and simple proclamation of the power of the Cross to save mankind from futility and despair. He is not arguing against scholarship or the serious study of philosophy, but against the pretensions of those who claim that the world can be put right by human wisdom. Man's real problem is that he is out of touch with God: the right relationship has broken down through man's pride and vanity. How can it be put right, how can man relate to God as he is meant to do?

The preaching of the gospel which claims to point the way to God looks like foolishness. But this is God's method, God's purpose. He chooses to reveal his deepest truths in ways that we should never have thought of for ourselves. Just as the prophets of old heard God speaking to them in unlikely ways – through the budding of a tree (*Jer.* 1:11f) or a pot boiling over (*Jer.* 1:13ff) – so he has spoken to us in our own time by a man on a Cross, a man who was nevertheless God's own Son and who was destined to be the Saviour of the world. This was not what the Jewish people expected or wanted – they looked for some spectacular proof that Jesus was the Messiah, not a carpenter crucified like a felon. The Gentile world on the other hand was looking for intellectual arguments which would prove to men that God exists and that they can know him with certainty.

So indeed they can, but it is by faith and not by logic. Both Jews and Gentiles in whose hearts God has kindled faith can see in the Cross the true power and wisdom of God. When they encounter the man on the Cross and realize the power he has to renew men's lives, they see that indeed this is God's wisdom as the means of the world's salvation, this apparent foolishness and weakness is real wisdom and real strength.

It was in keeping with what the world at large would call the foolishness of the Cross that God chose such ordinary people as the members of the Corinthian church to be his own – indeed less than ordinary, since they were drawn from the lowest ranks of society. But it was part of God's purpose to demonstrate that the Church would be based on different standards from those that prevailed in the outside world – not the strong and powerful but the weak and insignificant are to be his people. Thus they have no cause to boast of their own achievements, but only of what God has done for them. He has made them his own through no merit of theirs, but only through God's gracious mercy.

2:1-5 The message about Christ on the Cross
If we turn to the book of *Acts* we can read there (*Acts* 18) of Paul's first visit to Corinth to which he now refers. He had, as we have seen, gone there from Athens, where he had met with little success. Here he describes his arrival in Corinth in terms of bodily illness and mental depression (*1 Cor*. 2:3). We know that he suffered from a painful ailment (*2 Cor*. 12:7) which he speaks of as being meant to keep him from being too carried away by his religious experiences. He refers to it also in his letter to the Galatians in terms which suggest that it may have been some kind of ophthalmia (*Gal*. 4:13–15). But on his first visit to Corinth this was combined with some kind of nervous condition that made him tremble with fear. This could well be the uncertainty of not knowing whether his missionary technique which had been so successful in Asia Minor would be equally successful in Europe, among vastly different people. His unfortunate experience in Athens had not helped, and he had still not heard from Silvanus and Timothy, who

had been left behind in Macedonia to consolidate the mission at Thessalonica and Berea. It was not until Silvanus and Timothy arrived in Corinth with splendid news of the triumphant progress of the gospel in Macedonia that Paul recovered his confidence and threw himself wholeheartedly into the work of the mission in Corinth (*Acts* 18:5).

He recalls that time now, and reminds his readers that his message then had been the simple gospel of Christ and his Cross, without any of the embellishments of rhetoric and the orator's skill. It was the power of God evidenced in Paul's proclamation of the gospel that had awakened their faith, not scholastic brilliance.

2:6-16 God's wisdom

But there is another kind of wisdom, Paul goes on, which is different from the so-called 'wisdom' by which the Corinthians set so much store. It can only be understood by those who are spiritually mature. It is a wisdom which comes to us by revelation, not something which we can think up by ourselves. Paul calls it God's secret wisdom, which is in effect God's plan for the salvation of the world and how it is to be brought about. Like all Jews of his day, Paul thinks of this age as passing, to be succeeded by the age to come. The present age is dominated by evil powers and characterized by sin. When God brings in the new age it will mean the end of evil, and Jesus has already begun to destroy it. Christians thus live between the two ages. Christ by his Cross has defeated sin in principle but the victory is not yet wholly won. If the political and spiritual rulers of this world had understood that, they would not have crucified Jesus. This is the divine secret, the plan for the salvation of mankind.

But this secret purpose has been revealed to us by God's own Spirit. Each of us is known by his own spirit. Similarly God is known only by his Spirit and it is this Spirit that has been given to us. It is this that enables us to know God's gracious acts on our behalf. Thus what we say is no mere human wisdom but what we are taught to say by the Spirit of God. Only those who have God's Spirit in themselves can understand

God's word to us and can judge life's true values.

3:1-23 Servants of God

Paul now comes back to the situation at Corinth. Despite all that he has been saying about those who have the Spirit, he has to admit that the members of the Corinthian church fell far short of that standard. His readers were not – and still are not – living like men and women who have been seized by the power of the gospel. By their actions they are showing that they are very much citizens of this world and live by its standards. There is jealousy and quarrelling among them. They are proclaiming their allegiance to one or other of their leaders – some are for Paul, some for Apollos. Is this not simply behaving like men of the world?

After all, says the apostle, who is Apollos, and who is Paul? Both of them are simply the servants of God who instructed the members of the Corinthian church in the faith. They played the part that had been allotted to them. Paul had planted the seed, Apollos had watered the plant, but it was God who made the plant grow – God who had made the seed come to life. There is no distinction between the man who plants the seed and the man who waters it. God will reward each of them as he deserves. The missionaries are simply partners in the work of the mission, helping to further God's cause.

Paul now changes his metaphor from a garden to a building but the message is the same. The church in Corinth is one of God's buildings. Paul as the master builder used the gifts that God had given him to lay the foundations. Others will continue to build where he left off. But everyone who assists in the building of the congregation is responsible to God for what he does. There can only be one foundation, namely Jesus Christ. Whatever materials the builders use: gold, silver or fine stone, materials that will last: or wood, hay or straw – materials that will not endure; all of them will be required to pass the test of good building. Paul is of course speaking of the contribution of the various leaders and teachers in the Corinthian congregation. Some of them will be found to have made a gimcrack addition to the fabric which will not stand the test of time – that is, those whose teaching or leadership is confusing or erroneous.

This will all be made plain on the Day of Christ, the Day of Judgement, which Paul speaks of in terms of a day of fire which will test the quality of the building and destroy what is worthless. Paul means of course those elements in the life of the Christian community which are not true to the purpose and mind of Christ. Whatever features in the life of the congregation do not survive the fire of God's judgement will perish, and those who are responsible for them will see their work has been in vain. They will not themselves be destroyed. On the other hand, those who have contributed to the upbuilding of the community will be rewarded. Paul now speaks of the Church as God's temple, where his Spirit reigns. Anyone who sets about destroying the life of the Church, for example by creating divisions and factions, will be himself destroyed. No one should pride himself on his own wisdom or take an exaggerated view of the importance of one or other of the church leaders. They exist for the benefit of the congregation whose servants they are – but this is true of all experience, including death. All life's experiences are designed to be of service to the community, just as the community is the servant of Christ, as Christ is of God.

4:1-21 Apostles of Christ

Paul continues to defend himself and his colleagues. They are servants of Christ who have been made responsible custodians of the truth that God has revealed to them. The one thing that is required of such a servant is to be faithful to his master. He is not accountable to anyone else. Christ alone is entitled to judge him and that he will do when he comes again. Then the inmost thoughts of each man's heart will be revealed and God will judge him accordingly.

Paul cites Apollos and himself as illustrations of his point. What right have the Corinthians to discriminate between apostles – praising one and despising another? Whatever gifts they themselves may have – and Paul lists them in chapters 12 and 14 – they are gifts from God with no merit attaching to the possessors.

Although he insists a few moments later that he does not want to make his readers feel ashamed, the apostle proceeds to contrast the happy state of the Corinthians with the plight of the apostles, and Paul is obviously aggrieved. Apostles are despised, poorly clad and ill treated. They work hard to keep themselves alive, yet they are expected to endure persecution and insults and are treated by the world at large as trash. Paul is trying to stir the Corinthian church into a sense of awareness that their self-satisfaction is quite unjustified. If following Christ means hardship and humiliation for the apostles, the Corinthians ought to be sharing to some extent in similar suffering.

The apostle now makes it plain that he regards his own position in relation to the church members at Corinth as vastly more significant than that of their present guardians however many they be. (Paul speaks of 'ten thousand' which is of course pardonable exaggeration.) The people he refers to are not so much 'teachers' who give instruction. The Greek word is the same as the word Paul uses in *Galatians* 3:24 and means the slave who was put in charge of a boy until he was of an age to look after himself, taking him to school and generally supervising his behaviour. Paul on the other hand describes himself as the father of the Corinthian congregation, since he had been responsible for bringing the gospel to them and leading them to conversion. Let them follow his example, and to help them he is sending Timothy to them, his trusted lieutenant who will keep them on the right lines. Timothy had become Paul's companion on his second missionary journey and is always spoken of with the greatest affection. Paul often associates Timothy's name with his own in writing to the various churches, and indeed in the second letter to Corinth itself (1:1). Meanwhile some of the church members had been kicking over the traces and Paul, in promising an early visit to Corinth, leaves it to the Corinthian members to decide whether his visit is to be a painful one or a pleasant one, depending on whether they heed his words of admonition.

5:1-13 Immorality in the Church

Paul turns now to a specific case which has been reported
to him. It involves a member of the Christian community
living in an incestuous relationship with his stepmother –
something of which even pagans disapprove. This is
apparently still going on and the Corinthian church is
complacently taking no action. Paul demands the man's
expulsion from the congregation. Far from being proud
of themselves the Corinthians should be saddened that
such a thing could happen in a Christian group. Paul,
in far-off Ephesus, is nevertheless present in spirit at
Corinth and has made up his mind what is to be done.
The man must be solemnly excommunicated at a full
meeting of the local church. The language used here is
unfamiliar. The man is to be handed over to Satan for his
body to be destroyed so that his spirit may be saved
at the Day of Judgement. It was believed that within the
protection of the Christian Church God looked after
his own people. Anyone who was expelled from the
community was at the mercy of the demonic forces which
caused disease and death. His physical suffering was
designed to bring about repentance so that his soul would
be saved. If this seems harsh treatment, it should be
remembered that a young community was extremely
vulnerable and that incest was a heinous sin which must
be rooted out.

This is what Paul goes on to say, choosing as an analogy
the small piece of yeast which can leaven a whole batch
of dough. No community can allow itself to be poisoned
by even one defaulter, and it seems as if the Corinthians
were felt by the apostle to be treating the matter too
casually. The mention of leaven leads Paul to think of the
Passover, the great feast of unleavened bread. At
Passovertide it was the custom to remove all trace of
yeast from Jewish homes and use nothing but unleavened
bread during the festival, in commemoration of the
escape of the Israelites from Egypt at the time of the
Exodus. They had had to leave in such haste that they
did not wait for the dough to rise, but took it with them
as it was (*Deut*. 16:3; *Exod*. 12:33–34).

Yeast or leaven was used commonly as a synonym

for evil influences, and Jesus warns his followers to beware of the leaven of the Pharisees and Sadducees (*Matt.* 16:6, 12). Paul applies this idea to the situation at Corinth. The church members must get rid of evil influences which corrupt the whole community, for the Christian life is a perpetual Passover. Instead of the Passover lamb, which served to remind the Jews of their deliverance from human enemies, Christ had offered himself as a Passover sacrifice to deliver his people from sin and death. Paul calls on his readers to celebrate the feast with bread which is free from the old yeast of sin and immorality, bread that is pure and wholesome.

It looks as if Paul's original (lost) letter to Corinth (see p. 11), in which he had warned them against mixing with unsavoury types, had been misunderstood at Corinth, perhaps wilfully. After all, they may have replied, how can we avoid getting entangled with sub-Christian citizens in this pagan society? They had to go about their affairs, not in a vacuum, but in the world as it is. Paul now makes it clear that he was not speaking about normal pagans but about those who claimed to be Christians. Paul rounds off what he has been saying on this topic by calling on the members of the Christian community to put their house in order by shunning the company of anyone professing to be a Christian but behaving like a pagan.

6:1-11 Lawsuits against brothers

It seems as if another problem at Corinth was a passion for litigation. Instead of settling petty disputes among themselves, the Corinthian Christians preferred to take their fellow-members to court, leaving the decision in such matters in the hands of pagan magistrates. Have they forgotten, says Paul, that Christians will be called on to share in God's judgement of the heathen on the great Day, as it is promised in the book of *Wisdom* 3:7–8, *Daniel* 7:22 and confirmed by Jesus (*Matt.* 19:28; *Luke* 22:30)? They will also according to *Jude*, verse 6 and *2 Peter* 2:4 be called on to judge the angelic powers who in Jewish belief acted as guardians of the various nations. With this prospect, says Paul, it is plainly nonsense to make such heavy weather of little legal quibbles. Surely there must be someone in the Christian community to whom disputes between Christians can be referred without resorting to the courts and outside judges?

The fact that they go to law at all, continues Paul, is proof that they have not really understood the gospel. Have they forgotten what Jesus said about returning good for evil and putting up with injuries done to them instead of seeking redress? Far from that, they are actually defrauding their fellow-Christians. Make no mistake, says Paul as he lists a series of offences against God, no man will ever reach that blessed state of eternal life in the presence of God if he is guilty of these sins. He reminds them of their past black record before they became Christians, but this is no longer true. Through their baptism they have become new men and women, members of God's own people, with their sins forgiven and living now in the power of the Spirit.

6:12-20 Use your bodies for God's glory

One danger of Paul's insistence that Christ had freed men and women from the restraints of Old Testament Law was that some interpreted freedom as licence. There was an clement in the congregation at Corinth which maintained that Christians were free to do as they liked. Paul is strongly opposed to this misuse of the meaning of freedom. In theory a Christian had been liberated from the deadweight of crippling taboos, but, says Paul, that does not mean that every experience is beneficial, and there is the danger that one becomes enslaved to habits which are too powerful to discontinue. One is then no longer free.

Another line of argument from the Corinthians was that whatever seems natural must be right. If it is right to satisfy hunger when the need arises, is the same thing not true of the sex instinct? Is sex not a purely physical matter which is independent of our spiritual life and has no effect on our personalities? We have to remember that in Greek cities, above all in Corinth, the pagan temples were in effect brothels where unwanted girls were brought from baby farmers and used as temple prostitutes. Sexual intercourse with one of these sacred prostitutes was reckoned to amount to union with the goddess, notably Aphrodite. Paul takes the words of *Genesis* 2:24 referring to the marriage relationship in a literal and physical sense. When he says 'the two will become one body' he insists that this is not only true of a man and wife but of any casual relationship as well. This would mean that a Christian man who is part of the body of Christ violates this union with Christ by having sex with a prostitute. Our bodies are not our own to do what we like with them. Each of us is a temple of the Holy Spirit, made servants of God through what Christ has done. We must therefore use our bodies for God's glory.

7:1-16 Questions about marriage

Paul turns now to the questions that the Corinthian Christians have raised in their letter to him. Their first group of questions dealt with marriage. In his handling of these queries, Paul's whole attitude is coloured by the belief which prevailed among the early Christians that this world as we know it would shortly come to an end. So that while much of what he says here is eminently sensible and relevant, some of the positions he takes up are no longer valid. This is true of his first statement in which he advises against marrying at all. But for practical reasons, particularly in the highly sexual atmosphere of Corinth, Paul's recommendation is that marriage is the most satisfactory solution. Not only that, but a full sexual relationship is part of a husband and wife's Christian duty and there must be total equality between them. The husband's rights in this connection are no greater than the wife's. Any cessation of conjugal rights must be by agreement – and then only temporarily and for religious reasons. Paul is well aware that sexual urges that do not find fulfilment within a marriage will seek an outlet elsewhere. It is interesting in passing to note that Paul gives no encouragement to the Victorian notion that sex was somehow unladylike and that no respectable woman would admit to having the same urges and desires as men.

In his next words, despite his wise advice to those who are already married, Paul seems to be damning with faint praise the whole institution of marriage. He commends the state of being single and advises the unmarried, as well as widows, to stay as they are. If they cannot keep their sexual desires under control they would be well advised to get married: better that than be consumed with passion. We miss any mention of marriage as a lifelong companionship or of the pleasures of bringing up a family. However if Paul was convinced that the world would shortly be coming to an end, there was little point in taking this long-term view. It would appear that at the time of writing Paul was unmarried and living alone (verse 8). He may indeed never have been married, though this was unlikely in the case of a Jewish rabbi. More probably he was a widower and obviously for the kind of missionary life he had chosen there were advantages in being unattached.

In turning to the question of divorce in the case of a Christian husband and Christian wife Paul can speak categorically. Jesus himself had made it quite plain that it was not permissible (*Mark* 10:11–12). Marriage is a lifelong relationship. If it breaks down and a reconciliation is not possible, the couple must be content to remain separated. But what of the case of the Christian man who is married to a wife who is not a believer? Jesus had not said anything about this. The situation did not arise at that time in a purely Jewish setting. Paul recognizes that his own opinion had not the authority of a command from Jesus, but he gives it nevertheless. Provided the partner in such a mixed marriage is content to remain married, there must be no question of divorce. This is because the non-Christian husband or wife is accepted by God as belonging to his people by virtue of his (or her) marriage to a Christian. This also applies to the children of such a mixed marriage. Remember too that a mixed marriage is really a missionary situation. Who can calculate the possible influence for good upon a pagan married to a Christian? It may end in his (or her) ultimate salvation.

7:17–24 Live as God called you
Paul now reiterates his revolutionary doctrine, for a Jew, that racial differences mean nothing. It is the same

theme as he develops at length in his letter to the Galatians. If a man is born a Jew let him remain a Jew when he becomes a Christian, with the marks of his circumcision upon him. If he is born a Gentile, let him remain uncircumcised if he becomes a Christian, because circumcision means nothing. This ancient Jewish practice, which was meant to signify incorporation into the people of God, is merely a symbol. What matters is the obedience to God which it is designed to indicate.

Similarly if a man is born a slave, let him remain a slave if he is converted to Christianity. If the opportunity of becoming free arises, seize it. But what really matters is the relationship to Christ. A slave who becomes a Christian is in a deeper sense than any social status a free man, freed from the power of evil and liberated to the possibility of new life. By the same token a free man who becomes a Christian must become a slave, a slave to Christ. The paradox is that in the Christian life ordinary social standards are turned upside down. With the recent memories of slavery in the modern world – in the USA and Africa – it may seem that Paul is casual and even callous about matters which have bitten deeply into the souls of freedom fighters in the twentieth century – and rightly so. But let us not forget that slavery was not a colour problem in Paul's day and that slaves could achieve advancement and dignity in the ancient world in a way that the colour bar has made impossible. Paul was no racist.

7:25-40 Questions about the unmarried and the widows

The clue to the understanding of this next passage is in the first six words of verse 29: 'there is not much time left'. Once again what Paul has to say about marriage and celibacy is conditioned by the current belief among Christians in the imminent end of the world. This was to be preceded by a time of tribulation – 'the present distress' (verse 26). The thirteenth chapter of St Mark's gospel gives a vivid picture of wars, earthquakes, famines and other such disasters. Pregnant women and mothers of small babies are singled out as specially vulnerable. Paul takes occasion to warn his readers of

the effect this general upheaval will have upon family
relationships. Marriage and family ties produce complica-
tions that do not exist for the unmarried. Not only is
there the suffering of individuals themselves but the
agony of seeing their loved ones suffer as well. There
is also the additional consideration that marriage inevitably brings with it a variety of distracting problems
which can come between men and women and their
untrammelled service to God.

Paul's last point on the question of the rightness or
wrongness of marriage draws attention to a curious
custom in the early Church which did not survive.
Perhaps in protest at the low moral standards of the
pagans it seemed to some Christians that the best kind
of marriage was a spiritual marriage, i.e. a man and
woman lived together without, however, having any
sexual relations. This understandably involved them in
tremendous strain, and Paul says here that it would be
better for them to get married. If on the other hand the
man's self-control is great enough, they should not marry.
Either way no sin is involved, but Paul has a special
word of praise for those who can control their passions.

8:1-13 The question about food offered to idols
Paul proceeds now to deal with a matter he had been
asked about which on the face of it seems completely
out of tune with the modern world. Yet it establishes a
principle which is highly relevant for Christian conduct
and was a very real problem for people living in any
pagan city. Most of the meat that was for sale to the
public had previously been offered to the statue of one or
other of the gods or goddesses in one of the many
temples. In some cases the meat would be consumed on
some social or family occasion within the temple pre-
cincts. In other cases the carcases would find their way
into the meat market. It would be quite impossible to
know if a piece of meat came from an animal that had
been sacrificed to some pagan deity. This would not
upset the worldly wise in the Christian community who
scoffed at the idea that eating temple meat made any
difference, since idols represented gods that did not
exist. Paul agrees with them that there is only one God,

Creator and Father of all, and only one Lord, Jesus
Christ.

But there was a practical problem involved. Some of
the Corinthian Christians had been so conditioned by
their upbringing that they could not rid themselves of
the idea that in some way food dedicated to a pagan god
was contaminated and unclean. They felt guilty of sin.
Paul assures them that whatever food they ate has no
effect one way or the other on their relationship to God.
Their trouble was that they were over-scrupulous, and
misguidedly so.

But this lays especial obligation on the more enlightened
members of the community to see that they do nothing
to unsettle the simple believers. For example, if a
broadminded Christian, who knows what he is about,
attends a public banquet in a temple and is seen by his
more stupid fellow-Christians to be enjoying meat
which has been dedicated to a pagan god, will it not
encourage them to brush aside their scruples and eat
food which they still feel is tainted and commit what for
them is a sin? Paul declares roundly that if by eating
something which he knows to be harmless he becomes
guilty of leading astray simpler folk who will then be
plagued with a guilty conscience, he would become a
vegetarian forthwith. In modern society the analogy
would be to put temptation in the form of alcohol or
soft drugs in the way of an ex-addict. So out of this odd
problem in the ancient world Paul establishes the principle that knowing what is right is less important than
entering into the situation of others with sympathy and
understanding.

9:1-27 Rights and duties of an apostle

It comes as a surprise to find St Paul switching abruptly
from the question of eating 'temple meat' to defending
his status as an apostle. Some scholars think that we
have here part of a different letter. It is perhaps more
likely that Paul did not write – or rather dictate – his
letters in one piece. Especially with a fairly long letter
like this one, he may have had to dictate it in stages, as
and when he could free himself from other commitments,
or as and when a scribe was available. This would result

in a natural break, and between 8:13 and 9:1 some new thoughts may have occurred to him, or some further critical comments from Corinth may have come to his ears. At all events at this point we find him on the defensive.

Whatever others may say about him, Paul maintains that his qualifications to be an apostle cannot be denied. Not only his encounter with Christ on the Damascus road but the effectiveness of his ministry among the Corinthians themselves put his claims beyond dispute. As an apostle is he not entitled to the same privileges as other apostles? Can he not expect to be maintained at the expense of the Christian community and if he is married, like the brothers of Jesus and Peter, should not his wife also be chargeable to the church members? Is it only Barnabas and Paul who have to earn their keep?

Even the Law maintained that the ox which threshed the corn should not be muzzled, but should be allowed to eat its fill while treading out the corn (*Deut.* 25:4). Surely this includes human beings as well as animals. Should the ploughman and the harvester not reap some reward from their labours – much more so those who reap a spiritual harvest? But this, says Paul, is what he has steadfastly refused to do in case it should prove in any way to be a hindrance to the spread of the gospel. Not only do Jewish priests and Levites live off the offerings brought to the Temple, but Jesus himself has given instructions that his disciples who proclaim the gospel should be maintained by those who are ministered to by them (*Luke* 10:7). Despite all this, Paul has denied himself these privileges. He is under a divine compulsion to preach the gospel so that the question of financial reward does not arise. He is happy to work for nothing.

Paul now recalls his readiness to be everything to all men for the sake of winning converts. He has emphasized his Jewishness and addiction to Jewish customs (as in the case of Timothy – *Acts* 16:3). Similarly he has lived like a Gentile when among Gentiles for the sake of giving no offence by following Jewish practice. These are after all superficial matters. Obedience to the law of Christ is paramount. Paul concludes this passage in his letter by likening the Christian life to a race which demands intensive self-discipline, but where the prize is an eternal reward, or like a boxer who fights with determination and skill. To do this likewise calls for rigorous self-control.

10:1-33 Warning against idols
Despite all his efforts to keep himself spiritually fit, Paul is well aware that he might not pass God's searching tests and win his final approval (9:27). The Corinthians had apparently no such fears. They relied complacently on their incorporation into the people of God to keep them safe from his judgement. Accordingly Paul quotes some examples from Israelite history at the time of the Exodus to show that there is nothing automatic about salvation. Membership of the Church (the new people of God) will no more guarantee their freedom from temptation and sin than it did in the case of the old people of God who were punished in dramatic ways. They too had been protected by the pillar of cloud, symbol of the presence of God; they had been saved from death in the Red Sea, a kind of baptism; they had their sacramental bread, the manna which fell from heaven, and the water of life which Moses struck from the rock. According to Jewish legend the rock accompanied the Israelites on their journey through the desert, and Christian thought identified the rock with Christ, journeying with his people and sustaining them until they reached the promised land. Despite all these marks of God's favour, the old Israelites fell from grace in a variety of ways which Paul now enumerates, and they paid the penalty. Whether Paul thought those things had actually happened as they are recorded in the Old Testament is perhaps as doubtful as whether he thought the rock was literally Christ.

Paul's main point is that, whatever else it is, Old Testament history, the story of the people of God in the past, has been recorded for the guidance and admonition of the new people of God in the present critical time facing the end of the world as they knew it. The allusion to 'desiring evil things' (verse 6) refers to *Numbers* 11:4–6 where the people, despising God's gift of bread from heaven, clamoured for the more varied diet which they had enjoyed in Egypt. They also worshipped idols according to the story of the golden calf (*Exod.* 32:8) (verse 7) and committed fornication with Moabite women (*Num.* 25:1–9) (verse 8). They complained that God had led them into the desert and was leaving them to die, whereupon they were attacked by poisonous serpents (*Num.* 21:4–9) (verse 9). They revolted against Moses, their divinely appointed leader, and many perished in an earthquake (*Num.* 16) (verse 10).

Paul applies these lessons from Israel's past history to the Church in the present time. None of us is secure. All of us are liable to succumb to similar temptations – which are no worse for us than for past generations. But God gives us the strength to resist whatever temptations come our way. But as far as the Corinthians are concerned, they must keep themselves free from any contamination from idolatry. Paul still maintains that the idols in heathen temples have no real existence. But just as in the eucharist we share in the body and blood of Christ because we are all part of him, so by the same token by taking part in pagan sacrifices we become identified with the demonic powers represented by the pagan altars. There can be no communication between these two opposing objects of worship, and we confuse them at our peril. Paul is simply warning his readers, as he has already done in chapter 9, of the risk of playing with fire. There is no danger of contamination so long as they know what they are doing. They must be sensitive to the scruples of others even if they have no scruples on their own behalf.

11:1-16 Covering the head in worship

With the best will in the world, it is difficult not to feel that in dealing with the next topic Paul does himself less than justice. Yet it is impossible for a man to step out of his milieu – in Paul's case his rabbinical training, his Jewish male sense of superiority and privilege. Paul is true to himself and faithful to the mind of Christ when he writes to Galatia: 'There is no difference between Jews and Gentiles, between slaves and free men, between men and women: you are all one in union with Christ Jesus' (*Gal.* 3:28). This is the heart of the gospel. Compared with this, the sheer triviality of the purely local and ephemeral practices at Corinth with regard to women's attire and behaviour in church are not worth attention. Mercifully the good sense of women has rebelled against the fatuous literalism which persuaded some women to decorate their heads with handkerchiefs or similar eccentricities. Let us pass with relief to something rather more important. Even Paul himself has to fall back on the weak defence that women should have their heads covered in church because it is the done thing.

11:17-34 The Lord's Supper
In the miscellany of topics which Paul as a good pastor has to deal with, it comes as a surprise to us to notice that in the pristine purity of the early Church the sacred mystery of Holy Communion had in Corinth become a drunken debauch. Robert Burns had no illusions on this score in eighteenth-century Scotland, as readers of his 'Holy Fair' will well remember. But whatever abuses had crept into the observance of the Eucharist, we are indebted to the noisy and drunken Corinthians for the earliest authoritative instructions – based on the original practice of the Church – for the Institution of Holy Communion.

Notice that Paul does not claim to originate the teaching about the Lord's Supper which he is now passing on to his converts. He 'received' it and he is now handing it on. These are perhaps the most sacred and significant words in the whole gospel story. Here we are in the presence of the *mysterium tremendum*: 'THIS IS MY BODY'. How much heat and fire and sheer viciousness have gathered round this holy mystery!

12:1-11 Gifts from the Holy Spirit
In the next section of his letter Paul deals with spiritual gifts or gifts from the Holy Spirit. This topic has obviously been occasioned because he has been asked by his Corinthian correspondents for his advice. He begins by referring back to their days in paganism when, under the influence of strange powers not clearly understood, they would utter blasphemous cries such as 'a curse on Jesus'. This was dabbling in the borderline country between

religion and superstition – between the divine and the demonic. Paul lays down a guideline which is clear and straightforward. No one under the influence of the Spirit of God can utter a curse upon Jesus, and by the same token no one can acclaim Jesus as Lord unless the Holy Spirit inspires him.

Paul then goes on to a prolonged passage on spiritual gifts, insisting that whatever they may be it is the same power of God which is responsible for them. It may be that to one man is given the gift of understanding the underlying principles by which God manages his world; to another is given the power to communicate these principles to others. To one man is given the gift of the kind of faith that can move mountains; to another the power to heal men's bodies. Others are enabled to do miraculous things, others again receive the gift of proclaiming God's word, while yet others are able to discriminate between genuine messages from God and those that are spurious. Some are given the gift of speaking with tongues, that ecstatic type of utterance characteristic of Pentecostal worship, others are given the power to interpret the meaning of their utterances. To sum up, however, says Paul, it is all the work of the same Spirit who bestows these various gifts as he chooses.

12:12-31 One body with many parts

Paul now brings this line of thought to a climax. It is a bold conception of the unity of the Church dramatically pictured as the body of Christ. Just as a human body is made up of many parts, so is the body of Christ, and we are all parts of it. In Paul's day it was made up of Jews and Gentiles, slaves and freemen, who by baptism had become one body, empowered and sustained by the same Spirit. In our own day it is a much larger and wider fellowship, racially and socially mixed, but bound up into a single community by the presence of the Spirit. This is no paper membership but an organic unity. Each part of the body has its own role to play.

It may have been easier for those brought up like Paul with the Old Testament sense of racial solidarity rather than our own Western individualism, but it is something we have to learn. We are all members of one another, and the unifying factor is our common loyalty to Christ. We are all dependent on the supernatural help that comes from the Spirit and which alone can transform our mixed-up personalities into some semblance of a Christ-like life. For this, as Paul says to us here, we need one another's help, and no one is too unimportant to have a useful part to play in the community. Everyone matters, everyone counts, and our neighbour's successes and misfortunes are part of our own and are our concern.

Although we are all bound up with one another as members of the same community – the body of Christ – we do not all have the same function. Some of us are called to be apostles – like Paul himself. Others are destined to be prophets, that is, preachers engaged in the work of Christian evangelism. Others again are called to be teachers, with responsibility for instructing groups. Specific roles are set aside for those who are able to exercise supernatural powers, gifts of healing, moral counsel, spiritual direction, or ecstatic utterance. Not all will have the same gifts or will be called on to exercise them in the same way. Some are obviously more significant and influential than others – these are the gifts that are to be most earnestly desired. There is however one supreme gift which must be earnestly sought after, cultivated and prized beyond everything else – the gift of love.

13:1-13 Love

It is recorded that when this marvellous thirteenth chapter came up for consideration by the translators of the New English Bible the Director of the project, Professor C. H. Dodd, campaigned consistently, albeit unsuccessfully, for the retention of the Authorized Version's use of the word 'charity' in preference to the more popular word 'love'. His argument was, of course, that the word 'love' had been debased by Hollywood and that anyone who was a cinema-goer, which was true of most people at that time, would be less put off by the association of 'charity' with Victorian almshouses than by the modern identification of the word 'love' with sex.

This is Paul at his best in what has been described as the Beatitudes set to music. All the gifts of the Spirit which he has been referring to, and which are in all conscience important enough, are of no value in the life of a Christian if he does not have the God-given quality of love, which makes him truly part of the body of Christ. It is this that brings him into the right relationship with his neighbour and thus into the right relationship with God. Paul has been speaking of the inspired utterances of those who speak with 'strange sounds', who are caught up in heavenly ecstasies and speak of things beyond ordinary understanding. Paul will say more of this in the following chapter. But no matter how sublime its character, and how it impresses the listeners, it has no more value for the life of the Church or the individual Christian, if it is not motivated by love, than the noisy banging of gongs and cymbals in a pagan temple. This is equally true of great preaching, great knowledge and a faith deep enough to move the proverbial mountain. Without love, these things mean nothing. So it is with the sacrifice of all we possess, including our own bodies in martyrdom.

Paul then goes on to describe the characteristics of love. It might be a portrait of Jesus. Certainly no one else could match up to this standard. Unlike the words of the preacher – however moving – and the knowledge of the scholar, both of which are important, love has an eternal quality. In two wonderfully apt similes, Paul compares our present imperfect understanding of God, life and the ways of the world in general to the process of growing up from infancy to manhood, out of childish ways into full maturity and comprehension. Even now the best we can make of life is to see it as a reflection in a looking-glass. The real truth about God is still a closed book. But in the end, beyond this world, we shall know God as he knows us. In the meantime we live by faith, hope and love. These are the things that endure, and of these love is supreme.

14:1-25 More about gifts from the Spirit

Paul is clearly greatly concerned about the problems involved in what the *TEV* calls 'speaking with strange sounds', or more familiarly 'speaking with tongues'. Some confusion has been caused by the fact that in the

Old Testament the word 'prophesy' is used both of the clear incisive utterances of someone like Amos or Isaiah, for example, and the unintelligible babbling of the prophets of Baal. In the OT narrative in the Authorized Version the words used are 'they prophesied until the evening', which the New English Bible correctly translates as 'all afternoon they raved and ranted' (*1 Kgs.* 18:29).

This phenomenon was carried over into New Testament times – notably on the day of Pentecost. In his commentary (*Good News in Acts*) in this series, David Edwards gives an excellent account of what probably was involved in 'speaking with tongues' (pp. 34–7) and which is still a characteristic of Pentecostal church worship. Paul is critical of this, not because it is not a genuine religious experience, but because it is largely a private matter between the individual and God. The worshipper who is in the grip of the Spirit is unintelligible to anyone else. God will understand him, and some of those present at the service may be caught up in the same emotional rapture.

But for the enlightenment of the whole congregation, says Paul, it is far more important that what is said in church should be intelligible to others, for their encouragement and inspiration. The mind is as vital as the spirit in leading others in worship, and the ordinary members of the congregation must be able to understand what is being said and sung, otherwise it is all pointless. Paul himself had the gift of speaking with tongues, but he lays down the important principle that he would rather say five words that are meaningful to all present than thousands of unintelligible noises, cries of praise and prayer which no one else can share. Unbelievers may be impressed by taking part in a service where there is obvious sincerity, but it is more likely to leave them unmoved. Intelligible preaching is however more inclined to stimulate belief and awaken conscience.

14:26-40 Order in the church
Compared with the services of most modern denominations, church worship at Corinth would seem to have been disorderly and distracting. Anyone would appear

to have been free to utter as the Spirit moved him –
either singing a hymn, or making some doctrinal point,
or being caught up in some ecstasy, or explaining to the
rest what the ecstatic had meant. Paul is primarily
anxious that whatever is done should be done with
dignity and seemliness, everyone taking his turn. The
dead hand of Jewish male supremacy dictates that, even
in the Gentile world, women should be silent at church
meetings and services. Paul claims the Lord's authority
for this ruling. His last word is a plea for orderly worship
with tolerance of ecstatic utterance but with emphasis
on the preaching of the Word.

15:1-11 The Resurrection of Christ
Apparently – and not surprisingly – there was some
uncertainty and confusion about both the fact of Christ's
resurrection and also whether individual Christians
might hope to share in a future resurrection life. Paul
begins his answer by giving us what is the oldest evidence
for the resurrection of Jesus. He claims that this is what
he was told when he became a Christian, and that this
teaching is in accordance with what the Scriptures say,
namely that Christ died for our sins and was buried,
that he was raised to life on the third day and that he
then appeared to the apostles, beginning with Peter.
Finally he appeared to Paul himself on the road to
Damascus, an unworthy apostle because of his black
record as a persecutor of the Church.

When Paul says that these beliefs held commonly
among Christians were in accordance with the Scriptures,
in all probability he means the OT scriptures as a whole
but with special importance attached to *Isaiah* 53. This
particular chapter had a profound effect on the thought
of the early Church. They were certain that when Isaiah
had spoken of the Servant of God who was to come, who
would be humiliated and vilified, who would bear his
sufferings with patience and without reproach, who
would accept all this as God's will for him, and regard
his own death as a sacrifice on behalf of others, he could
have been speaking of none other than Jesus. But God
would vindicate him and exalt him and he would be the
means of bringing the world to the knowledge of God.

15:12-34 Our resurrection
It is not surprising that every facet of this prophecy was
pondered over and that it came to mean more and more
to the Church, especially after the Easter events which
confirmed what Isaiah had foretold. For it was not only
the Resurrection of Christ that was at issue but the resurrection at the last day of all Christian believers. The one
depended on the other. Paul comes back here to the
Old Testament idea of corporate personality or racial
solidarity. We are all as sinful human beings identified
with Adam, and subject to death. Adam is the symbol
of our unredeemed human nature, which is mortal. But
by faith-union with Christ we shall share in Christ's
Resurrection when he comes. Paul sees this pictorially
as involving ultimately the rule of Christ over everything,
including death, and the final stage of salvation will be
God's dominion over everything including his Son.

15:35-58 The resurrection body
Most of this fifteenth chapter takes us into areas of
thought which are unfamiliar and perplexing. Apart
from the historical evidence for Christ's Resurrection at
the beginning of the chapter, Paul's argument is tied up
with thought-forms which are time-conditioned and
impermanent. There is also the problem of how much we
should treat literally and how much is metaphor. The
New Testament as a whole does not encourage speculation
about what happens after the body dies. We are left at
best with certain guidelines which are based on Christian
convictions. We cannot expect a programmatic description of what is in effect a different order of being from
anything we have known. Paul in this chapter gives us
certain clues based on his deeper perception of what is
involved than any of us could pretend to have. First of
all, there is no question of our physical bodies being
restored to their former state after death. Our bodies
disintegrate, but there is continuity between what we
are now and what we shall be after resurrection. Our
personalities remain distinct and recognizable, but they
are transformed to fit their new mode of existence.

16:1-4 The offering for fellow-believers
From the contemplation of these mysteries Paul comes
back to the particular issue which lies very close to his
heart – the raising of money to send to the mother church
in Jerusalem for the relief of their poor.

16:5-24 Paul's plans and final words
He hopes to visit Corinth for a long stay on the way. He
puts in a good word for Timothy and ends with greetings,
a personal note from himself, and a prayer in Aramaic
(the language used by Jesus himself) for the coming of
Christ as Lord of the Church and the world.

PAUL'S SECOND LETTER
TO THE CORINTHIANS

1:1-11 Paul gives thanks to God

If we read straight on from the end of Paul's first letter
and into his second letter we get a rather misleading
picture of the situation, for between the two letters he
had had to pay a short visit to Corinth – a much less
pleasant one than his original visit – and in addition he
had to write the Corinthians a stiff letter. He describes
the visit as unhappy (*2 Cor.* 2:1) and speaks of the pain
which writing that letter had caused him (*2 Cor.* 2:4.)
But there had also been trouble in Ephesus (*2 Cor.* 1:8)
where he was now working, so serious that Paul speaks
as though he had been at death's door. Whether this was
illness or persecution we cannot tell. What is clear,
however, is that he had not had his sorrows to seek
either in connection with Corinth or at Ephesus. Yet
nothing could quench Paul's faith and trust in God.
Had not Jesus triumphed over all his afflictions? So,
despite all that has happened, Paul's first words in this
letter are words of thanksgiving to God.

1:12-2:4 The change in Paul's plans

There has obviously been much criticism of a change in
Paul's plans. He promised at the end of his first letter
to pay a long visit to Corinth (*1 Cor.* 16:5-7). This he
has not done, and he has now to explain why. Someone
in the Corinthian church has obviously committed some
act of indiscipline, which reflects not only on Paul but
also on the Christian community in Corinth as a whole.
We are not told what it was. But the man has been
subjected to church discipline and now Paul is asking the
Corinthian congregation to let bygones be bygones.

2:5-11 Forgiveness for the offender

It would be useful at this point to consult a map of the
Eastern Mediterranean (p. 124). Paul is located in and
around Ephesus (in Asia Minor). On hearing bad news

from Corinth he crosses the Aegean to see for himself what the trouble was. This was the 'painful' visit to which he refers in *2 Corinthians* 2:1 and it would not have been too difficult to fit in since it was a busy route with plenty of shipping. It must have been after this visit that the obscure act of indiscipline occurred, perhaps a personal insult to Paul or one of his associates, such as Timothy. Deciding not to visit Corinth again in the meantime, he wrote what he calls the 'painful' letter referred to in *2 Corinthians* 2:1–6, which many scholars think has been incorporated as chapters 10–13 of *2 Corinthians*.

2:12–13 Paul's anxiety in Troas
This letter was sent to Corinth by the hand of Titus, and it was about this time that Paul was in danger of his life at Ephesus (*2 Cor.* 1:8–10). Leaving Ephesus on his way to Macedonia (*2 Cor.* 1:16), he had to sail north to Troas. He expected to find Titus there with news from Corinth but, failing to contact him, he went on himself across the Aegean to Macedonia. There at last he met Titus and got good news from him about the situation in Corinth (*2 Cor.* 7:5–16), following which he wrote Second Corinthians or at any rate the first nine chapters, if *2 Corinthians* 10–13 are part of the 'painful' letter. All this, though slightly confusing, gives us a valuable insight into the day-to-day life of the apostle at this time and the strains to which he was subjected.

2:14–17 Victory through Christ
Titus, who is not mentioned in *Acts*, is referred to in *Galatians* 2:1–3 as being with Paul in Jerusalem, and he is said to have been responsible later for organizing the church in Crete. But here he is brought into Paul's narrative as the bearer of the good news about the Corinthian church, a topic which Paul returns to in *2 Corinthians* 7:7 and which made up for the troubles he encountered in Macedonia. Paul begins now on a new topic, the work of an apostle, which continues up to the end of chapter 6. He starts by picturing Christ as a victorious general with incense burning along the route of his triumphal progress. But, as Paul points out, this can either be the deadly poison of judgement on those

who are inclined to turn their backs on the gospel and risk perdition or, on the other hand, for those who are on the way to salvation, the road is open to eternal life.

3:1-18 Servants of the new covenant

It would appear that some people had come to Corinth bringing letters of commendation from churches elsewhere, but at the same time casting aspersions on Paul. His answer to that is to claim that he needs no letters of introduction, for the Corinthian church itself is his best letter of commendation, written on his heart. The success of his mission to Corinth is not only his best recommendation to the world at large, but something that abides in his heart as a perpetual reassurance.

The thought of a letter written on the heart, both for the benefit of the outside world and of the apostle himself, leads inevitably to the contrast between the old covenant and the new. The old covenant was written on tablets of stone (*Exod.* 31:18) whereas, as Jeremiah had foretold, the new covenant would be written on men's hearts (*Jer.* 31:33). Under the new covenant there would be no need of written instructions, for the Spirit would give men guidance directly to the heart. This is a new kind of direct relationship, life-giving in that the Spirit not only shows men what they are to do but gives them power to do it. The written law which showed men what they must not do gave them no power to avoid sin, and therefore brought upon them the ultimate punishment of death.

Still dwelling on the contrast between the two covenants, Paul thinks again of the giving of the Law under Moses at the time of the Exodus (*Exod.* 24:16–17) when, as we are told, not only did the splendour of God's presence overshadow the scene, but Moses' own face shone with the reflection of that splendour. He had to put a veil over his face since the Israelites could not bear the sight of God's glory. But that was a glory that faded, and the veil was also designed to save them from seeing the vision disappear. Even to this day, says Paul, the Jewish mind is closed to the truth, only to be opened to it when the Jews turn to Christ. We, on the other hand, reflect God's glory with no intervening veil, and are transformed into the likeness of Christ.

4:1-15 Spiritual treasure in clay pots

This, says Paul, is the marvel of the apostolic commission. We know that it is not our own merit but God's mercy which gives us power, so we never lose heart. Our lives are open to God and to our fellow-men. If there is any obstacle to belief, any 'veil' which hides the glory of God from men, it comes from the power of evil which dominates the human scene and blots out the face of Christ. The light of God's revelation coming through Christ is the Good News that the apostles proclaim, the message of which they are but servants.

Paul compares the chances and changes of the life of an apostle to the fragile impermanence of a clay pot which is often used to hide treasure. The clay pots are of themselves worthless, but how valuable are their contents! We know, he says, that we apostles are likewise vulnerable and perishable and that the treasure we preserve is not of our creation. So, no matter what dangers and hardships we have to endure, we never totally despair. As apostles, Paul goes on, we walk with death, in constant peril of our lives. This means sharing Christ's death, yet at the same time we share his risen life, for we are being daily inwardly renewed. What are these passing troubles that afflict us compared with the hope of resurrection which awaits us?

4:16-5:10 Living by faith

This passage, like that in *1 Corinthians* 15 dealing with the same subject – the Resurrection Body – is beset with the same difficulties, the main one being that Paul knew no more than we do about life after death. Yet people found the subject as fascinating then as in our own day, and presumably some of the Corinthians had raised the question. Various explanations have been offered to solve the problem raised by these controversial verses. But it is doubtful whether they leave us any wiser. As in the case of *1 Corinthians* 15, the most we can hope for are the inspired reflections of the apostle based on his deeper faith and understanding than our own. Basic to his time-conditioned views is the conviction that what matters is our relationship to Christ. This is something that the death of our bodies does not affect. What happens to us after death – where we go and how we exist – is a matter of secondary importance.

5:11-6:13 Friendship with God through Christ

Paul now comes back to the conduct of the apostles. They are obviously under attack, particularly Paul himself. In reply Paul claims that all the apostles are concerned only to serve God and the community. This is the example that Christ has left and which they must follow. At one time – presumably before they became Christians – they, Paul included, had judged Christ by human standards. But now they are new men, changed by God into his friends and charged to make others God's friends. What separates men from God is sin, but this is certainly not God's intention. His concern is rather to bridge the gulf and bring men into the relationship he had planned. This can only happen if men recognize that they are guilty. Paul now says that, although Christ was without sin, he entered into man's situation, accepted the consequences of sin, including death, which as Paul believed was the punishment for sin, and thereby restored the broken relationship.

At the beginning of chapter 6 Paul strikes the note of urgency so common in the NT. There is not a day to lose. God has chosen to make this the time for reconciliation, the hour of salvation. Accordingly the apostles go out of their way to commend themselves and their cause by their endurance of hardship. In this way they show that they are truly God's servants. They have as Paul says been beaten, imprisoned and mobbed, they have been overworked, sleepless and starving. Yet they have consistently shown themselves to be God's servants by their behaviour – their patience, kindliness and love. Their only weapon is righteousness, both in attack and defence. They accept equally honour and dishonour, praise and blame. They are treated as dishonest, yet it is the truth that they are speaking. They are the unknown men whom everybody knows. They should by all accounts have been dead but they still live on. Despite their sufferings they still survive. Although they have their sorrows they have also their joys. Although they have no money themselves they have made many rich. They seem to have nothing but in fact they own the world. Paul appeals to his Corinthian readers to be as open with him as he has been with them, to show some of the same affection for him as their father in God as he feels for them.

6:14-7:1 Warning against pagan influences

There is a sudden and surprising change of topic at this point which has led many scholars to believe that we have here in 6:14–7:1 an independent short letter interpolated into the main substance of *2 Corinthians*. This could happen easily enough if the few papyrus sheets involved had been displaced, and inserted at a slightly later date at this point. The simplest explanation is to think of this fragment as the lost letter referred to by Paul in *1 Corinthians* 5:9, his first letter to Corinth, which apparently dealt with the very topic which is referred to here, the danger of associating with unbelievers. There is the further point that the apostle's words in 6:11, 13 about being open-hearted connect logically with the appeal in 7:2: 'Make room for us in your hearts'. The point of Paul's insistence here on avoiding too close relations with pagans springs not so much from a desire to keep the Christian community separate from the rest of society, as to guard against the deterioration of moral standards. When Paul speaks of light and darkness living together he is obviously referring to mixed marriages between pagans and Christians. He is not advocating divorce in such a case, but rather warning against the danger of embarking on such a marriage. Paul reverts to the points he made in *1 Corinthians* 10 about Christians taking part in social occasions in pagan temples and warns his readers of the danger of playing with fire, using Old Testament quotations to support his case. He pleads with his readers to keep themselves clean in body and mind and calls for total consecration in the fear of God.

7:2-16 Paul's joy

Paul now takes up again the thread of his narrative. If we are right in thinking that 6:14–7:1 has been a fragment of his first letter to Corinth, referred to in *1 Corinthians* 5:9, his opening words in 7:2 follow on naturally from his last words in 6:13: 'Make room for us in your hearts'. He speaks of his pride in the Corinthian church and of his joy at the good news about the church in Corinth which Titus had brought to him in Macedonia. He needed all the comfort that Titus could give him. He speaks of troubles, quarrels and anxiety. Titus had however assured him of the loyalty and affection which the Corinthian church felt for Paul, which gladdened his heart.

He refers again to the 'painful' letter which he has already mentioned in *2 Corinthians* 2:1–6 and which had been occasioned by the obscure act of indiscipline which had caused him so much grief. He does not now regret having sent it, because it has brought about a change of heart and led to a reconciliation between the apostle and his Corinthian friends.

8:1-24 Christian giving
Paul now goes on to speak of the collection he is organizing among the Gentile churches on behalf of the poor in the mother church in Jerusalem. This task lay heavily on his mind. It may seem odd that so little is said of this in the narrative of the book of *Acts*. It is not so surprising, however, when we reflect that Luke was writing his history of the early Church at a time when many of the issues that plagued Paul's life as a missionary were no longer of burning importance. But in Paul's own letters, written when the collection was one of his major concerns, there are many indications of the great significance he attached to the enterprise.

He saw it not merely as an act of charity and compassion to help the sorely tried members of the Jerusalem church, who were not only poorer than their wealthier fellow-Christians in Gentile cities, but who may never have recovered from the sharing of their possessions which dated back to the earliest days of the Church just after Pentecost (*Acts* 2:44–45).

More significant in Paul's mind than the practical effect of monetary help – which at best would be temporary – was the demonstration to the Jerusalem Jews and to those Jewish Christians who shared their narrow views on such matters as the sanctity of circumcision, and the paramount importance of the dietary regulations in the Old Testament, that Gentile Christians who did not share these views were eager to show their solidarity with their Jewish Christian brethren as followers of the same Lord despite their differing practices. Finally in Paul's reckoning the collection was a means of uniting the young Gentile churches not only with the mother church but with each other in a common cause and common sacrifice.

Paul's missionary efforts had been bedevilled by the suspicions and antagonism of Jewish Christian extremists who went out of their way to stir up trouble in the Gentile churches, notably in Galatia, by insisting that Gentiles who wished to become Christians must first become Jews by acceptance of Jewish restrictive practices. This to Paul was anathema, and his noble plea in his letter to the Galatians in defence of the freedom of all Christians to enter the Church on equal terms, whether they had come from a Jewish or Gentile background, is one of the great advances in Christian thinking. Paul felt that this principle was the only real safeguard of Christian unity, and the only certain defence against the Church's developing into two distinct Christian movements, Jewish and Gentile.

It is this disastrous prospect which induces Paul to dwell at length on the collection. The Corinthians had begun to contribute in the previous year but it would seem that their enthusiasm had faded. To encourage them, he quotes the example of generosity set by the churches in Macedonia – most likely the congregations at Thessalonica, Philippi and Berea – which Paul had himself founded. He reminds them now of the story of the manna in the wilderness at the time of the Exodus (*Exod.* 16:18) where, by sharing what they had, there was enough for everyone.

Titus had turned out to be an enthusiastic ally who volunteered to go to Corinth to assist in the collection. He was to be accompanied by an unnamed but prominent missionary who has been nominated for this task not by Paul but by the churches at large. Paul is anxious to

allay any possible criticism on the part of his opponents
that he is collecting money for his own benefit. It is
obvious from what he says that he is under constant
scrutiny from his critics and that he is doing everything
in his power to give no grounds for complaint. Accordingly he strengthens his team with the addition of another
emissary to Corinth also chosen by the churches and not
by Paul.

9:1-15 Help for fellow-Christians

Continuing with his advocacy of help for the Jerusalem
church, Paul now commends the readiness of the Corinthian church to take a full share in the collection. This
is for the benefit of the Macedonian churches, whose
generosity he has already commended to the Corinthians
– an age-old technique of money-raisers everywhere!
To be on the safe side, however, he sends the Macedonian
delegates in advance so that, when Paul eventually
arrives in Corinth, the collection will have been made.

Paul rounds off his appeal with some words of general
exhortation. Whatever they give will not be given in
vain. It is not only a gift to their poorer brethren in
Judea but an expression of their thanksgiving to God
for all his goodness. More than that, it will be a means
of bringing the two sections of the Church together.
Jewish Christians and Gentile Christians will be united
in gratitude to God for Christ, and for this further
evidence of his grace.

10:1-18 Paul defends his ministry

A problem arises at this point affecting the last four
chapters of Second Corinthians. Paul has been dealing
at some length with the arrangements for making a
collection for the mother church in Jerusalem. Suddenly
he switches to something quite different, and we find
him defending himself against unnamed opponents who
have questioned Paul's authority, maligned his character,
and caused him considerable unhappiness. As we have
seen, it is not unusual for Paul to jump from one subject
to another, as we do ourselves in writing letters. What
is surprising, however, is the change in tone between the
first nine chapters of this letter (2 Cor. 1–9) and the last

four chapters (*2 Cor.* 10–13). Whereas he has been writing
in terms of friendship and affection, he now without
warning becomes vehement, aggressive and almost
hostile.

Many attempts have been made to explain this, but
it is difficult not to feel that Second Corinthians is made
up of two different letters, chapters 1–9 and chapters
10–13. Some scholars go further and find evidence of
even more than two letters – or parts of them – in this
single composition. This would be quite in keeping with
the general character of Biblical writings, which tend to
be composite in any case, but we ought to have very good
grounds indeed for splitting up a book of the Bible into
various 'original' documents. Here, however, there does
seem to be a balance of evidence in favour of separating
the last four chapters of Second Corinthians from the
rest.

If we do that, we find ourselves confronted by a different Paul from the man who has been full of praise
and encouragement for the Christian community in
Corinth. Instead we find the apostle seething with
righteous indignation. He is accused of being two-faced
– weak and ineffectual when he is with them and bold
and aggressive when he is away from them. It seems most
reasonable to explain this contradiction by thinking of
these last four chapters as part of this angry or 'severe'
letter to which Paul refers in 2:3 and 7:8, and to place it
before chapters 1–9.

Paul does not identify his opponents in this 'severe'
letter, but from his comments we can build up a picture
of what sort of people they were and of the trouble they
were causing. Paul is accused of moral weakness and of
acting from worldly motives. His reply is that, however
weak he may be personally, he has the power of God behind him. He distrusts the clever arguments put forward
by his opponents: they are specious and false. His own
authority rests on the fact that, humanly speaking, he
was the founder of the Corinthian church, whereas his
opponents wrongly claimed to be apostles with special
authority over the Corinthian church members. He will
see to it that when the Corinthians come to their senses
again and recover their loyalty to their founder, these

intruders will be punished. They have come into another missionary's territory boasting in no time that they have been responsible for the conversion of the whole area to Christianity and that they are the founders of the Corinthian church. Paul on the other hand proposes to develop what he has begun in Corinth and thereafter to proceed to new areas further afield. This may be a reference to his proposal to go on to Spain after he has paid his proposed visit to Rome (*Rom.* 15:23, 24).

11:1-15 Paul and the false apostles
Paul now mingles irony with sarcasm as he trounces these bogus 'apostles' who have done so much damage in the congregation he has so carefully built up. He reveals more of the seriousness of their undermining of the original gospel he had proclaimed in Corinth. They had shaken the foundations so painstakingly laid by Paul by commending a travesty of the gospel and preaching a different Jesus. (Could this be a Jesus who was no more than a great prophet?) He likens himself to a father presenting his daughter to her bridegroom – in this case the congregation is the bride pledged to her husband Christ. He thinks of the false 'apostles' as corrupting the purity of the bride, as in the story in *Genesis* 3 Eve was led astray by the serpent.

Paul is very sensitive to any suggestion that he was making money out of his preaching at Corinth. Apparently this is what was being maintained by the false 'apostles'. Paul, however, denies this hotly. He got all the financial help he needed from his friends in Macedonia.

11:16-33 Paul's sufferings as an apostle
Then Paul launches out into a magnificent torrent of self-justification – apologizing for talking like a boastful fool as he does so. He can match anybody's record with respect to the purity of his ancestry (his opponents were apparently making much of their Jewish credentials) and can outstrip anyone's record of service of Christ and of sufferings in his cause. He has indeed much reason for boasting. In his account of his various judicial punishments, attacks by various mobs and a variety of mishaps on sea and land, he tells us of many disasters

which are not mentioned anywhere else. Paul is not likely to be exaggerating or claiming to have suffered more than what was in fact true. His opponents would be quick enough to convict him of lying. He rounds off his catalogue of misfortunes with a reference to his escape from Damascus over the city wall in a basket. He seems to mention this as the crowning indignity of his career and Luke even refers to it in *Acts* 9:25. But when all is said and done, Paul's concern for all the churches has been his greatest burden.

12:1-10 Paul's visions and revelations

Paul turns now to his spiritual experiences, notably a remarkable vision which he no doubt refers to here because the false apostles had been boasting about their own. There is no doubt that he is talking about himself, although he disguises it as the experience of 'a certain Christian man'. He dates this as having happened fourteen years before, which would put it before the start of his missionary journeys (*Acts* 11:26). He felt himself being carried up to the very presence of God – though he is still not clear whether it was vision or reality.

What he is quite clear about, however, is the painful affliction – the famous 'thorn in the flesh' – which he regards as God's way of keeping him from spiritual pride. All sorts of suggestions have been made as to what this may have been. There is no way of knowing for certain, but malaria or eye trouble seems most likely. At all events Paul has found in his weakness the strength which comes from God.

12:11-21 Paul's concern for the Corinthians

Paul keeps coming back to the false 'apostles'. It obviously is something that he cannot put out of his mind, although he is aggrieved that he has to keep harping on the same theme. The Corinthians should be springing to his defence instead of his having to make his own case. His only failure, and here he speaks with bitterness, was that he did not ask them for money like the rest. But as their father in God he does not expect them to provide for him, any more than any normal parent would do. He reminds them of his record when he was among them, not only the more spectacular signs of an apostolic ministry, such as healing of minds and bodies, but in his patient endurance of hardships and hostility.

Paul now speaks of an impending third visit to Corinth. It is difficult to identify this visit. This confusion is one of the problems of the Corinthian correspondence, but it should not concern the non-specialist reader. Paul's message in these letters to Corinth is independent of whether he paid one visit or ten – or none. He takes a realistic view of his coming visit. He paints anything but a rosy picture of what he expects to find when he gets to Corinth. The last two verses of chapter 12 cover the whole gamut of human frailty despite Paul's best efforts.

13:1-14 Final warnings and greetings
The apostle ends his letter on a sombre note. He has been accused by his detractors of weakness. He will now show his authority in terms of punishing the offenders. Although as a Christian he shares Christ's human weakness, he also shares his divine power. If the Corinthians really believe that Christ is in them it will show itself in their Christian conduct. His fervent hope is that they will take themselves in hand so that when he comes to Corinth there will be no unpleasantness. Paul ends his letter with a plea for harmony and a blessing.

CORINTHIANS TODAY

When the New English Bible appeared, many people threw up their hats in the belief that now at last the major difficulty of reading the Bible had been solved. No longer would we be frustrated by the archaic language of King James's day. The use and meaning of words had changed over the intervening centuries and, in particular, young intelligent people felt that much of the Bible had become unintelligible to modern minds, and that a clean sweep should be made of the old words and ideas which had become out of date. Individual translators such as James Moffatt, whose brilliant version of the Old and New Testaments had opened up new vistas for countless readers eager to find a Bible meaningful in their own day, suffered from the disadvantage that this was after all the work of only one man and not, like the Authorized Version, the work of many expert hands. The New English Bible seemed to sidestep this difficulty, since panels of scholars drawn from various denominations collaborated in the work.

But it soon became clear that a translation which used modern English was not the whole answer to the problem. When the scholars had exercised their skill in giving us a fresh, up-to-date translation, there was still the difficulty for ordinary readers of bridging a gap of two thousand years in the case of the New Testament and considerably more in the case of the Old Testament. Men literally lived in a different world in Bible times. It was not just that television, speedier travel and endless gadgets had made life easier and more convenient for modern man. It was more than that. People thought in a different way, especially in the Western world. There was undoubtedly much in common between the peasant communities of the East in Bible times and the present-day life of villagers in Africa, India, China and in Asia as a whole. On the other hand, what point of contact is there between the city-dweller in a high-rise flat with his car, telephone, colour TV, his canned foods, camera and central heating, and the poverty-stricken inhabitant of a mud hut on the edge of the jungle, scratching a living out of barren soil to be divided among a veritable army of children and relatives, most of whom will never leave their tribal areas, far less venture into foreign lands?

Yet they have all something in common, whether they live in New York with its teeming millions or in one of the scattered villages of equatorial Africa. They are all the children of God, black and white, brown and yellow. They will be suckled at their mothers' breasts, they will grow up, fall in love, get married and have children of their own. They will know heartbreak and happiness, they will have their joys and sorrows, their moments of exultation and depression, they will go through the whole range of human experience from hope to despair. This is what binds mankind, despite differences of race, colour and social status, into one great fellowship, the brotherhood of man. This ideal has become slightly tarnished since its hey-day last century, but it is still a valid hope and faith in the minds of millions. It is certainly what the Bible teaches us to work for and pray for.

Today's English Version, the translation of the New Testament which is being used for this series of commentaries, takes us a stage further than the *New English Bible* in the direction of giving the people a Bible in the language of our time. But why should commentaries be necessary? The answer is that with the best will in the world Bible translations, however accurate and popular they be, do not go far enough to bridge the gap between our own day and the time when the New Testament was written. It is not just that the conditions of modern life are different but also that we think differently, use different expressions and have to face many new problems about which the writers of the New Testament knew little or nothing. We need not only a good and readable translation of the Scriptures, and a commentary on the text which brings out its meaning, but also an attempt to bridge the centuries and relate the message to life as we have to live it, and to emphasize the passages in which the New Testament writers have something directly to say to us now.

Paul's letters to Corinth are a case in point. We can see from even a casual reading of these letters that there are many issues on which the apostle Paul has something to say from which we can learn and profit. But there is much else which passes us by. So let us look at these letters again and try to pick out some of the issues which Paul felt to be all-important and which we can still feel to be of major concern in our own day. There is, for example, right at the beginning of his first letter a consuming passion for the unity of the Church. He is not primarily concerned with organizational unity. He had founded himself, or through his associates had sponsored the foundation of, small groups of Christians up and down the Mediterranean world. One of these happened to be in Corinth and so he addresses himself to that particular situation. But the idea of divisions within the community of Christ's people is to him unthinkable. They have one Lord and Master and to him alone they owe allegiance. Preachers, missionaries, apostles – whoever they may be – are united with the ordinary members of the Church in a common commitment to Christ.

But when Paul speaks of commitment to Christ he is thinking of the crucified Christ and the power of his Cross. It is here that Paul would part company with those who see Christianity as merely a code of behaviour or a subject for discussion. For him on the other hand it is the power of new life and the gateway to freedom. To the world at large the Cross may be nonsense, as it was for the Greeks in Paul's day. The New Testament writers and Paul in particular never insisted on a single answer to the question that still disturbs many. They rather insist that Christ died for our sins according to the Scriptures, no doubt having in mind principally the picture of the Suffering Servant of God in *Isaiah* 53, who gave his life for others and whose death was to be the means of bringing the world to the knowledge of God. When we ask how this was brought about, Paul is content to call it God's 'secret wisdom' (*1 Cor.* 2:7). But he has no doubt that no other message is worth proclaiming and that no other message can save the world.

As we have seen, doubtless Paul's humiliating experience with the philosophers of Athens affected his preaching of the gospel at Corinth. It was not necessarily his last word on the subject. His letter to the Romans, to say nothing of his later letters written from prison, stresses different facets of the gospel, but it would not be far from the truth to say that whatever terms he used, at Corinth or elsewhere, his message was essentially to hold up the crucified Christ before men's eyes and let the effect of that work on their minds under the guidance of God. Paul sees the Good News as primarily God's power to change men's lives. He himself had been changed from being a vindictive, intolerant little Jewish rabbi into a large-hearted, great-souled friend of humankind, capable of awakening love and devotion in the most unlikely people. If God could do this for him he could do it for all men, if they would commit themselves to him and let Christ take over their lives.

There is a magnificent passage at the end of the third chapter of his first letter to Corinth (*1 Cor.* 3:21–23) in which Paul dramatically outlines the place and status of the ordinary Christian. He has described the members of the Church variously as God's field, God's building, God's temple. Then he rounds this off by making an astonishing statement, expressed almost casually: 'Actually everything belongs to you . . . this world, life and death, the present and the future: all of these are yours, and you belong to Christ and Christ belongs to God.' And remember that Paul is writing to people, many of whom would be described as the offscourings of Corinth. But this and no less is the high calling of all who have accepted Christ as their Lord – Jews and Gentiles, rich and poor, old and young.

Most of us, whether we like it or not, have to spend our lives and earn our living in cities. Paul likewise grew up, lived and worked in cities not unlike those in the modern world, and had to face many of the same problems as we have to cope with. Unlike Jesus, who was a countryman born and bred, and who drew on the countryside and the village for his illustrations and teaching material, Paul takes his local colour from city life. We see him against a background of endless traffic and crowded streets, to say nothing of the frequent athletic games and sporting fixtures. So that while Christianity began among the quiet hills and villages of Galilee, it was in the teeming ghettos and noisy markets of the Middle East that it spread and flourished.

This has certainly something of vital importance to say to us today. If Christianity could make such an impact on a world not basically different from our own, why is it not doing so now? Let us not be too despondent, however, and let us give thanks to God that despite all the hostile forces at work in the world – the onrush of materialism, the superficiality of modern culture, the deadening effect of the mass media, the decline in individual craftsmanship and the sheer complexity of present-day life – politically, economically and socially – there is still a live witness of faith in countless homes, and in small groups in the old world, the new world and above all in the Third World. This is a heartening testimony to the perennial power of the gospel to touch men's hearts and to keep the Christian faith a living power in men's lives. Sometimes people despair of Christianity ever making progress in an overcrowded world. They look back with longing to the placid tempo of life in former times, when the parish church was the centre of every village community, where the country rector was the father of his people, when moral standards were high, manners were better, society was stable and everybody knew his place.

But did this idyllic state ever exist in England? It is certainly not the picture we get from John Wesley of eighteenth-century England, nor is it the picture we get of first-century Corinth from the apostle Paul. He is not even writing about the pagan masses in the city, but of the small group of baptized Christians, who would appear to have been quarrelsome, irreverent, complacent about flagrant immorality in their midst, litigious and greedy. Yet these are the people for whom Paul gives thanks to God and whom he praises for their devotion to Christ.

Paul accepted the fact that we are by nature sinners and that only the gift of God's grace keeps us from disaster. But he found, like all the saints since his day, so much that was lovable in the rough and tumble of ordinary human beings that his heart was big enough to pray for them and to feel himself bound to them in fellowship with Christ. With such a warm human sympathy we can understand why it was that he attracted to himself – as Jesus did – many whom the more orthodox moralists in the Christian community regarded with disfavour or direct disapproval. Contrary to what has popularly been maintained about him, Paul was a lover of men. He had thrown off his Pharisaic self-righteousness on the road to Damascus and had emerged from that overwhelming experience a new man in Christ.

In these letters to Corinth we find a Paul who is not a dogmatic theologian or a moral rigorist, but a deeply concerned father in God immensely involved in the problems of a particularly difficult group of Christians. In his moving self-portrait (2 Cor. 11:21ff), in which he describes what he has suffered as a missionary, he speaks of his daily concern for all the churches. This is no empty claim. Every page of his letters – not least those to the Corinthians – speaks of his passionate and single-minded devotion to his far-flung flock. He agonized over their failures, rejoiced in their achievements, and shared in their struggle to maintain their faith.

We cannot pretend that the printed words of these letters can serve as a substitute for the direct personal impact that Paul must have made on his Corinthians. The letters would be read aloud at church meetings and at public worship more or less as they are today. But with most of the congregation there would be the added realism of words and phrases which they had actually heard. They could picture the apostle himself, supply his characteristic gestures and recall his voice. We have, alas, no such advantages. How then can we make these letters come alive for us twenty centuries later? We can at least picture Paul as he was. He is described in the second-century romance called *The Acts of Paul and Thecla* in such unflattering terms that they ring true: a short bald-headed man with a hook nose and bandy legs, probably at this time about fifty to sixty years old. We know that he dictated his letters to a scribe – which was the normal practice – so we may think of him pacing up and down a room, sometimes with a letter in his

hand to which he was replying. The disjointed character of
his letters was probably the result of his eyes catching
sight of a new point which he proceeded to deal with.
The letters were written in Greek which was the world
language of that time, used and understood by educated
people throughout the Roman Empire. Occasionally
Paul employs an Aramaic word or expression, since this
was the local language of Palestine, Hebrew being used
in the services of the synagogue for the Old Testament
readings.

SOME OF PAUL'S THOUGHTS

Before turning to the question of how best to use the
letters of Paul in our own day we should perhaps ask
ourselves why we should read them at all. Part of the
answer is obviously because they reflect the life of the
Church in its earliest days. We can learn from them what
were the major issues which concerned the first Christians
and what sort of answers Paul gave to the questions
which puzzled the first generation of Christians as they
still puzzle us today. But what authority should we give
them? As we have seen, not all that Paul said can be
taken at its face value, for example what he has to say
about women having their heads covered in church
(*1 Cor.* 11). This is clearly as unimportant as whether
women today should wear skirts or slacks in church.
Paul makes a clear distinction between his own opinions
and what he considers to be direct commands of Christ.
These latter must be taken as binding. There can be
no higher authority than the words of Jesus (e.g. *1 Cor.*
7:25).

The plain fact of the matter is that we may not think
of or speak of the words of Jesus in any ordinary human
category. There is an undoubted mystique about this.
Jesus was no ordinary person – he was not merely a
prophet, a major figure in the Old Testament galaxy,
but someone who made claims such as no other man had
made and did things that no other man has done. Paul
does not come into this category. Jesus is unique and the
whole Church acknowledges him as Lord and Saviour.
Paul at best is the greatest of Jesus' followers. But he was
so deeply committed to Jesus, so much of a man in

Christ, that the mind of his Master speaks to us in most of what he says.

But let us not expect the impossible. Paul is writing letters, not theological treatises. Like anyone else's letters there is bound to be a fair amount of triviality – travel arrangements, personal details which concern nobody but the individual himself. Yet above and beyond that, there are many issues in these letters which have perennial significance and are of relevance for our own day. Let us look at some of them, taking them in the order in which they appear in Paul's letters.

1 Cor. 1:8 'He will also keep you firm to the end, so that you will be found without fault in the day of our Lord Jesus Christ.'

There are frequent references in Paul's writings to what was apparently a powerful element in the preaching of the early Church – the impending return of Christ. In some of the Christian congregations it would seem to have grown into an obsession as, for example, at Thessalonica. From Old Testament times there had been a growing conviction that history would end in the triumph of God over the hostile forces of evil, a Day of Judgement on the whole world and its peoples. By New Testament times the judge had become identified with Christ. The ascended Christ would return to claim his own faithful people and punish his enemies. There were many aspects of this belief but the basic conviction was, as the Creed maintains, that 'Christ will come again with glory to judge the living and the dead'. This has always been firmly embedded in the faith of the Church and is still a cardinal element in Christian belief. Opinions differ as to how much this future hope is to be understood literally, but there can be no doubt that for Paul and the early Christians the climax of history was not far off.

This is not surprising. It has always been held that when Messiah came evil would be routed. Now Messiah had come but evil was still triumphant. Yet God's purpose could not be defeated. Christ would return to gather his faithful people and found his kingdom. The resurrection, Pentecost and the rich outcrop of supernatural happenings encouraged the belief that the day could not be long delayed. When the end of the world did not come as they expected, the first Christians thought through the problem once again and came to the conclusion that they had misunderstood the scriptural promises, and that a long uphill climb lay ahead of the Church before the time was ripe for the consummation of God's purpose.

1 Cor. 6:12-20 'Use your bodies for God's glory.'

This is a particularly difficult issue in our own day. Improved contraceptive methods which were presumably designed to control the birth rate are now accessible to people of all ages, married and unmarried. This puts an enormous strain on young couples who in previous generations were protected and supported by a generally accepted code of sexual behaviour, which regarded sex outside marriage as not only a violation of publicly accepted standards but also, in the case of those who took seriously the demands of Christian conduct, sinful in the sight of God.

There are many who would say that young people today behave no differently from what has always been the case. Statistics of sexual relations outside marriage are notoriously unreliable. Despite the greater freedom allowed to public discussion of sex, erotic magazines, film censorship and so forth, it is quite impossible to generalize on the effect of this new freedom on the actual behaviour of young adults – to say nothing of the not-so-young, married and unmarried.

No doubt in Paul's day the temple prostitutes constituted a special problem in the cities which has no exact parallel in the modern world, since they had the approval of religious custom. But for Christians higher standards are required. Paul lifts the discussion on to the highest level when he speaks of our bodies as temples of the Holy Spirit and parts of the body of Christ. In this case there is a direct obligation on the Christian to 'avoid immorality' (verse 18).

1 Cor. 7:10-11 'A married woman must not leave her husband ... and a husband must not divorce his wife.'
On this question of marriage and divorce Paul takes his stand on the words of Jesus (*Mark* 10:11-12). But once again in our permissive society the restraints of a stable family background are lacking. The word 'divorce' trips off the tongue in a casual context that would have been unthinkable last century. Husband and wife would rather have faced a lifetime of wrangling, bitterness or poisonous silences than expose themselves to the scandal of legal action. But surely the impact of a broken home upon young and impressionable children is more damaging than a clean break and a fresh start with another partner? The multi-marriages of the 'fast set' make a mockery of any kind of home life in a Christian context. But it would almost seem as if common sense, in recognizing that the breakdown of a marriage relationship is at least as valid a ground for divorce as adultery, is more humane than Christian principles. Yet Jesus was clearly no legalist. His ultimate criterion is love, and where love has died the marriage bond has become a hollow shell. He would surely not condemn a couple to a lifetime of misery when there was a possibility of a fresh start with someone else.

1 Cor. 9:1 'Am I not an apostle? Haven't I seen Jesus our Lord?'
When the Twelve – now reduced to eleven by the death of Judas – set about filling his place, a criterion of eligibility was to be that he should be one of those who had accompanied Jesus during his ministry in Galilee (*Acts* 1:21-22). Paul obviously did not qualify under this head, but the question has often been asked whether Jesus and Paul had ever met. Paul certainly claims here to have seen Jesus. But it is more likely that he is referring to his encounter with the risen Christ on the road to Damascus, which led to his conversion as recorded in the book of *Acts* (chapter 9). Jesus and Paul were roughly the same age, and Paul could have been in Jerusalem in Passion week. It would be unlikely, however, if this had been so, that Paul would not have taken

sides violently one way or the other at the time of the crucifixion, and would have referred to the fact on one of the occasions when he was defending his claim to be an apostle.

1 Cor. 9:22 'I become all things to all men, that I may save some of them by any means possible.'

Paul might at first sight be accused of being a trimmer, a mere timeserver who suited his message to his audience – a politician rather than an evangelist. Yet it is obvious that he courted unpopularity and suffered bodily injury for the truth he believed in. He is referring here to compromises on matters which he regards as relatively unimportant. When in the company of Jews, he would conform to Jewish restrictive practices in matters of food, rigid sabbath observance, and such like, which he had now come to see were of no significance one way or the other. Similarly in Gentile circles he would transgress jealously guarded Jewish traditions which as an orthodox Pharisee he had at one time regarded as sacrosanct. What he would not compromise on was his commitment to Christ as Saviour and Lord.

1 Cor. 11:25 'This cup is God's new covenant sealed with my blood.'

Although this is not an original thought of Paul but of Jesus, we may consider it here.

One of the striking features of the Bible is the way themes and patterns keep recurring, linking the Old Testament with the New. One of the most distinctive of these is the covenant–principle. This involves basically a relationship between two parties who may be equals – as in the case of legal transactions – or far from equals as in the case of covenants between God and man. These are of course the significant covenants from the Biblical point of view. God makes a covenant with Noah by which Noah, representing mankind, is guaranteed a stable and ordered world, while in return he undertakes to respect his neighbours' rights. A further stage is reached when God makes a covenant with Abraham, which constitutes him as the founding father of the people of God. The great covenant in Old Testament times is

between God and Moses, by which keeping the Law
becomes incumbent on Israel, and in return God undertakes to protect his chosen people provided they keep
the terms of Old Testament Law.

Later, the prophet Jeremiah looks forward to the time
when written laws will be replaced by the law written
on men's hearts, a new relationship based on man's
obedience and God's forgiveness. It is this new covenant
that Jesus refers to in his words at the Last Supper,
quoted by Paul for the guidance of the Corinthian church.
He speaks of his impending death as the seal of a new
relationship between God and man, and Paul sees each
eucharistic celebration as recalling Christ's sacrificial
giving of himself for men.

**1 Cor. 14:15 'I will pray with my spirit but I will pray
also with my mind.'**
It is worth emphasizing that Christianity, guided by our
Lord himself, has always been a religion, as Luther put
it, for men with a head upon their shoulders. Its appeal,
in other words, has been to men's reason. Paul leaves
us in no doubt that, while he did not underestimate the
part played by our emotions in worship, he put more
value on the part played by our minds. It is important
that this should be stressed at a time when the irrational
in music and the arts is being commended as a new
revelation. One suspects that much that is said and written
about new art forms is spoken with tongue in cheek,
and we may hope that this phase will pass. But it is
more serious when some young people succumb to the
hypnotic effect of freak religions which are outside the
main streams of traditional forms of worship. Jesus
cautioned against what the Authorized Version calls
'vain repetitions' or 'babbling' in prayer, which is
quite different from the frequent use in worship of the
Lord's Prayer, which he then proceeded to teach his
disciples. The repeated utterance of the name of God in
some foreign tongue is not prayer in the Christian sense.

**2 Cor. 1:9 'We felt that the sentence of death had been
passed against us.'**
Part of the difficulty of understanding Paul's letters is

that we seldom know exactly how much of the particular
situation to which Paul refers at any given time was known
to the recipients of the letter. Time and again, details are
lacking which would elucidate a puzzling sentence or
paragraph, simply because the readers of the letter were
so much more in the picture than we are. This reference
to a recent crisis in the apostle's life is a case in point.
We do not know if it was mob violence, or severe illness,
and all sorts of guesses have been made. It is unlikely
to have been the same occasion to which Paul refers in
his first letter as fighting with 'wild beasts' at Ephesus,
where he was at the time (*1 Cor.* 15:32), since the Corinthians knew about that already, and this on the other
hand appears to be something of which they did not know.
At all events he despaired of his life, and from the various
hints he gives us it would seem to have been a severe
illness. What is more important is the conclusion the
apostle draws from his recovery, namely that God alone
can save and can bring life out of death, and that the
intercessions of faithful friends evoke God's healing
power.

**2 Cor. 4:5 'For it is not ourselves that we preach: we
preach Jesus Christ as Lord and ourselves as your servants
for Jesus' sake.'**
Paul speaks from the heart in this second letter to Corinth
as nowhere else in his letters, and here is one of his
great utterances as he describes his role and that of the
other missionaries. In face of opposition, setbacks, and
rival claimants, he sets out the glory of being a minister
of the gospel. The man himself drops into the background,
leaving Jesus in the centre of the stage. He is Lord, and
the missionaries are merely his servants (or slaves), and
not merely slaves of Christ but of all who are committed
to Christ. It is through these weak, imperfect mortals
that God communicates the knowledge of himself that
is to be found in the works and words of Jesus.

2 Cor. 5:10 'For all of us must appear before Christ, to be judged by him, so that each one may receive what he deserves, according to what he has done, good or bad, in his bodily life.'

Not surprisingly the thought of death, particularly his own, bulks more largely in Paul's mind as he faces crisis after crisis. In one sense for him this is a matter for rejoicing, because death for the Christian means to be at home with the Lord (verse 8).

But the thought of death is also a challenge to the Christian to live as Christ would have him live in face of his judgement on us. We shall all have to give account of our lives, whether we have tried to live in obedience to God's demands or whether we have tried to please God less than to follow our own inclinations. The possibility of being at the end of the day rejected by God must not be ruled out, and Paul includes himself among those who may suffer this fate (*1 Cor.* 9:27).

2 Cor. 5:19 'Our message is that God was making friends of all men through Christ.'

These words in the heart of one of the great passages in Paul's letters are in *TEV* a pale shadow of earlier translations and of what Paul originally said. This is not just because the English of the older versions is more robust. It is also a more accurate rendering of the Greek. Something along the lines of 'God was in Christ reconciling the world to himself' brings out the powerful thought of the apostle. He means more than 'making friends'. It involves God's forgiveness. This was the message of which the missionaries were ambassadors.

2 Cor. 6:4 'In everything we do we show that we are God's servants.'

Later in this letter (chapter 11) Paul apologizes for boasting 'like a fool'. In this passage here he might be accused of the same thing. He speaks of what he has endured, and also of his 'purity, patience and kindness' (verse 6). This is all true, but we should perhaps not expect Paul to say so. We should remember, however, the circumstances, and that he is writing passionately in defence of his fellow-missionaries and not just of himself. There is also the added strain of his battle with the 'false apostles' – pretentious rivals who were doing their best to discredit Paul and his supporters. Their attacks were unscrupulous and unjustified, and it is this sense of the unfairness of their campaign against him that makes him explode with indignation.

2 Cor. 8:20 'We are being careful not to stir up any complaints about the way we handle this generous gift.'
One of the fascinating sidelights on Paul's character is his shrewdness and practical good sense in business matters. One would perhaps have thought that a man who could write of being transported into the place of heavenly mysteries, so wonderful that he could barely tell whether it was an actual experience or a vision (*2 Cor.* 12:2–4), would be the last man to be so aware of people's suspicious natures where money is involved. Paul's record and motives were always beyond reproach, but he knew how men's minds worked and that the slightest suggestion of possible misuse of church funds could do untold harm to his whole missionary enterprise. Hence his elaborate plans to check and cross-check the administration of the collection for the Judean Christians.

2 Cor. 11:8 'While I was working among you I was paid by other churches.'
Paul was particularly sensitive about his own financial affairs. He refers to this frequently throughout his letters. The reason was that there were so many charlatans posing as philosophers or peddling new brands of religion or practising various types of black magic, and preying on a credulous public in the process, that Christian missionaries tended to be lumped together with the rest. As far as possible Paul tried to be self-supporting by working at his trade of tentmaking – and indeed keeping his fellow-missionaries as well (cf. *1 Thess.* 2:9; *2 Thess.* 3:8–9). On occasion he allowed wealthier congregations, such as that at Philippi, to send him gifts of money, but that was the exception.

2 Cor. 11:22 'Are they Hebrews? So am I. Are they Israelites? So am I. Are they Abraham's descendants? So am I.'

Stirred to violent protest by the pretensions and claims of the 'false apostles', Paul justifies his own record, apologizing at the same time for boasting like a fool. Apparently his opponents emphasized their Jewish ancestry, so Paul claims his Hebrew descent. Moreover he claims that he is an Israelite – a member of the people of God – and a descendant of Abraham. These three amount more or less to the same thing.

2 Cor. 11:24 'Five times I was given the thirty-nine lashes by the Jews.'

Paul's catalogue of his sufferings includes natural disasters, some of which, as previously noted, we hear of only in this letter, and judicial punishments as well as mob violence. Forty lashes was the maximum synagogue punishment – in this case presumably for Paul's Christian propaganda – and one stroke was usually remitted as an act of mercy. Roman punishments were administered with rods, no doubt in Paul's case for disturbance of the peace in a Roman colony such as Philippi (*Acts* 16:22).

2 Cor. 12:2 'I know a certain Christian man who fourteen years ago was snatched up to the highest heaven.'

The Greek text actually says 'as far as the third heaven'. Paul is not using scientific language but the language of apocalyptic which distinguished various levels of heaven. In Paul's day the third heaven seems to have been commonly regarded as the highest level and was used as a synonym for Paradise.

2 Cor. 12:7 'I was given a painful physical ailment.'

This reference to what is generally alluded to by its more common description as 'a thorn in the flesh' is still a puzzle. Paul speaks of it as God's way of preventing him from being too carried away with his visions. The usual explanation is that it was malaria or some kind of eye trouble. But there seems to be much to be said for the more recent suggestion that it was an impediment in his speech. This stutter or whatever it was may have been the result of ill-treatment on a particular occasion.

HOW TO READ THESE LETTERS

Behind all such specific problems of interpretation in these letters to Corinth lies the biggest issue of all, namely how are we to use them with the greatest profit to ourselves? There is obviously no golden rule about this. Different minds have different methods. Some of us may favour the old and well-tried method of reading a chapter a day before going to bed, and letting a particular thought linger in our minds as we fall asleep. Others find that, if they are the kind of people who are early risers, a few minutes in the morning before getting up are the most fruitful, especially if we begin and end with a short prayer.

But not everyone can do this either morning or evening without finding their mind wandering, and we may have to school ourselves to concentrate on what we are reading, often without success. It is here that biblical commentaries perhaps perform their most useful service. They are not designed to answer all the questions that we should like to put to them. Commentators are only human, and what strikes one commentator as important might not strike the reader in the same way. But they do on the whole try to face up with honesty to what they feel to be the questions that readers of the Bible find most puzzling, and if they do not succeed in this they may well spark off in the reader's mind trains of thought which lead him to suggest the answers for himself.

Many people find it more helpful to join a Bible study group. Those of us who have done this have usually found that although some of the discussion seems to be a waste of time, and does not appear to be leading anywhere, an odd remark from some unexpected quarter turns out to be the start of a fruitful line of enquiry and leads to unexpected discoveries. In this connection a word of caution might not be out of place. The traditional pattern of group Bible study was to choose a leader for the group who had taken the trouble to prepare himself by doing a bit of homework beforehand – reading and thinking about the proposed passage on his own, consulting one or more commentaries, filling in the background and trying to see the passage in its wider context.

After all, any biblical commentator spends a considerable time finding out from a wide range of previous commentators what has been said over the years by his predecessors. He also brings to his Bible study his own theological training, knowledge of the original languages, a love of the Bible, and a real desire to communicate something of what the Bible has come to mean to himself. The most recent trend towards what is called 'unstructured groups', groups without any particular leader, where each member is expected to say whatever comes into his or her head after about five or ten minutes of reading through the passage, as often as not ends up in embarrassing silences, or in the most loquacious member dominating the discussion with little profit to anyone, including himself.

With the growing movement away from a full-time ministry towards part-time ministries, we are not only recovering a valuable element in the life of the early Church, but also bringing fresh points of view into the organized ministry, and drawing on the expertise of many who have had experience in business or industry in ways which have usually not been open to conventionally trained clergy. This is an undoubted gain for the life of the congregations, but it places an obligation on the Church at large to see that these part-time ministers are soundly schooled in the basic teaching of Christianity. Despite the understandable desire of each denomination to ensure that its part-time ministers are given a grounding in the history and distinctive doctrines of that particular branch of the Church, the Bible is the foundation of all sound Christian education.

CORINTHIANS IN ITS BIBLICAL SETTING
It is of interest and of some value for those who propose to exercise any kind of teaching and preaching ministry to have some idea of the main beliefs of the great world religions – Buddhism, Islam, Hinduism and the rest – especially in view of our recently created multi-racial society. But it is far more important to be firmly grounded

in the contents of the Old and New Testaments, which have inspired and influenced Western civilization as no other book has done. The Bible tells the story of how a faith that had its birth among the hills of an out-of-the-way corner of the Roman Empire spread through the towns and cities of the Near East, North Africa and Europe with a promise of development into the still-to-be-discovered lands of America and Australia.

We can respect and admire much that the other great faiths can teach us, but Christ's commission to his first disciples was to be witnesses for him 'in Jerusalem, in all of Judaea and Samaria and to the ends of the earth' (*Acts* 1:8). Christianity is a universal religion and it has followers in every corner of the globe. It is not the private possession of the English-speaking peoples, although we often misguidedly speak as if it were. But what cannot be denied is that the Bible has had an immeasurable influence on our own heritage. Victor Hugo said: 'England has two books, the Bible and Shakespeare. England made Shakespeare, but the Bible made England.' And we may add 'together with the English-speaking world'. This is not the main reason for reading the Bible, but it is certainly not the least important one.

The main reason is of course that the Bible is a unique book – the story of our origins, the title deeds of our faith, and the source of all that we know – and can know – of the historical person of Jesus. These words of J. K. S. Reid in *The Authority of Scripture* are worth recalling: 'The authority of the Bible reposes in the fact that, in statements some right and some wrong, and in practical application some of which is disputable and some even more dubious, a unified witness is borne to Him who is at the centre of the Gospel.' This eminently sound and balanced evaluation of the authority of the Bible for us in the twentieth century avoids the pitfalls in which so many students and inexperienced teachers of the Bible find themselves.

The days of verbal infallibility are gone. We can no longer take refuge in the magical view that in some mysterious way the text of the Bible has been protected from all human error. Its writers were fallible mortals whose memories sometimes played them false, who did not always understand what they had heard and seen, but they were honest men who did not wilfully distort the truth, and who were deeply conscious that they were engaged in no ordinary task, but were recording God's acts for the salvation of the world. We cannot study any part of the Bible in isolation. We must always see each piece of writing – gospel, epistle, psalm or prophecy – as part of the total pageant or panorama of God's revelation of the truth about himself and us.

Above all we must recognize, as F. W. Robertson said, that 'Scripture is full of Christ. From *Genesis* to *Revelation* everything breathes of Him, not every letter of every sentence, but the spirit of every chapter.' Everyone will have favourite texts that he has found more than ordinarily helpful, and similarly each of us has his favourite biblical book. For many it may be the *Psalms*. More perhaps will settle for a gospel, *St John* or *St Luke* most likely of all. I have often thought that, although there is much to be said for knowing one book of the Bible really well, there is the same danger as faces the preacher who has only one theme or, worse still, only one text – however striking and fundamental it may be. Such a text could be: 'God loved the world so much that he gave his only Son, so that everyone who believes in him may not die but have eternal life. For God did not send his Son into the world to be its Judge, but to be its Saviour' (*John* 3:16–17). This says something that takes us right to the heart of the gospel, but it does not say everything, otherwise there would be no need to print the whole Bible.

THE STORY OF THE ACTS OF GOD

The truth is that we need to have grasped the message of the Bible as a whole, and to have some idea of the variety of its contents, so that we can see it as a book about life in all its richness and its possibilities. For it is not a mine of information for archaeologists and ancient historians, far less for astronomers and biologists. If this had been recognized last century in the heat of the science versus religion controversy, much less bitter wrangling would have ensued. The legacy of that un-

necessary confrontation is still, on the part of the
scientists, a distrust of the Church's integrity.

For the Bible is a book about God and man, and above
all about man's relationship to God and to his fellow-
men. There are many ways of expressing this, but one
of the most helpful ways has always seemed to me to be
to picture the Bible as a divine drama, the story of the
Acts of God. It divides neatly, as it happens, into three
acts with a prologue and an epilogue. The prologue
(*Gen.* 1–11) sets the stage for the three acts of the drama,
painting a contemporary picture of man in the world
he has been given to live in. Endowed with the good earth
to develop and use for his enrichment and given guidance
on how best to do that, he chooses instead to run the
world for his own selfish ambitions, stopping at nothing
to gain his ends – violence, deceit, lies, murder – the
whole gamut of human folly defaces the fair picture of
God's design for his creatures. Man's pride and wilful
disobedience distort God's plan for his advancement.
The world turns sour, and man, adrift from God, finds
himself at odds with his Creator and with his fellows. All
of this is sketched in a series of little pictures that read
like fairy tales but are in fact full of profound theology.

But God is not content to leave mankind to its own
devices. His plan is to rescue man from his folly, and this
he does by choosing a small and insignificant people,
the Jews, to be a pilot scheme for the renewal of the
life of the world. Act I of the drama (*Gen.* 12 to the
end of the Old Testament) tells how this people, beginning with Abraham, and leading on through Moses and
the prophets, were schooled in the truth about themselves
and the life we all have to live. They had to learn through
their mistakes and misadventures that honesty, kindness
and compassion are the only bases for a wholesome and
prosperous society, because these virtues reflect the
nature of the Creator, and because it is his will that men
should live together in brotherhood and mutual service
and not in hatred, violence and cruelty, ending in self-
destruction. All this had to be learned by trial and error,
and from the experience of the Old Testament people
the world at large was meant to profit. But God's plan
foundered on human greed and corruption.

So when all else failed God sent his Son, to do for men what they were unable and unwilling to do for themselves. Act II of the divine drama (the four gospels) tells of the coming of Christ into human life to show us what God is like and how he wants us to live. This is the heart of the Bible and the clue to its understanding. These four accounts of the enigmatic prophet from Nazareth each came from a different Christian community and each underlined the different facets of Jesus' life and teaching which appealed most strongly to the respective writers. Added together they give us a picture of a unique person – a normal man who said such things about himself and his role in the world as no other man had ever said, who had a strange power to change men's lives from being self-centred, irresolute and tearful into being bold and purposeful disciples; who was able to restore health and sanity to those who turned to him for help, and who gathered around him a committed band of followers who became convinced that he was the long-awaited Messiah of Old Testament psalm and prophecy, and that he had the power to turn death into life.

Act III of the divine drama (the rest of the New Testament after the gospels) shows us this small body of men embarking on a fantastic adventure – nothing less than to win the world for their new-found faith. It meant hardship, persecution, and for some of them death. But they did not flinch. Since his countrymen had disowned Jesus, first rejecting his message, then eventually handing him over to the Roman authorities for the horrible punishment of crucifixion, the incredible had happened. First one then another became convinced that their Jesus was not dead but gloriously alive and would be with them, as he had said, until the end of the world. Strengthened by this knowledge and comforted by their Master's presence, what had they to fear? As one of them, a late convert from Tarsus in Asia Minor, a Jew with a vision which reached to the boundaries of the inhabited world, said at his trial: 'the Lord stayed with me and gave me strength' (2 Tim. 4:17). And Paul was only one of the host of martyrs who gave their lives for their faith.

It is a glorious and moving story which the New

Testament tells in Act III – an act which is still being played out wherever the followers of Jesus throughout the world seek to infuse his spirit into the life of mankind and reshape society in accordance with his teaching. But this is not the Bible's last word. To round off the drama we are given an epilogue – the book of *Revelation* – where in glimpses of unsurpassable glory the ultimate victory of God's cause is firmly asserted. The end of the battle for the souls of men is not in doubt. Christ will win, evil will be routed, and God will dwell among his people for ever.

This majestic vision is the note on which the Bible ends. In the divine drama it has not flinched from telling us the truth about ourselves, showing us the morass in which we flounder through our pride and self-will, but holding out the promise that God's purpose will finally prevail. Such an inadequate sketch,* which does little justice to the rich variety of biblical thinking, is the background against which we must see every component part of the Bible, whether it be a gospel, a psalm or an epistle. And it is likewise the background into which we must fit prophets, apostles and the countless men and women, named and unnamed, who make up the story of the people of God.

PAUL'S ROLE

Among the characters in the divine drama St Paul plays no mean role. A Hebrew of the Hebrews, proud of his Jewish heritage, jealous of the traditions of his people, he was none the less prepared to jettison them all for the sake of his allegiance to Jesus, whose willing slave he had become. No event in the whole history of the Christian Church can rank in importance with the conversion of St Paul. It is beyond the compass of ordinary mortals to guess at what might have happened had Paul been enrolled on the other side. He could not have played a minor part. A man of his boundless energy, self-dedication, and outstanding intellect could, humanly speaking, have wrecked the prospects of Christianity and stifled it at birth, had he devoted his life to its extermina-

* I have given a more extensive account of this total picture which the Bible contains in *The Bible Story* (Collins, 1970).

tion with the same passion as he devoted to its further-
ance. But in the providence of God this was not to be,
and from the moment on the road to Damascus when this
venomous, cruel little rabbi was changed into a 'man in
Christ', the course of history was given a new direction.

Paul was a fantastic person who has never commended
himself to everybody. We have noted already in these
Corinthian letters, among the most personal of his
writings that have survived, how much they reveal of
the man himself. Who but Paul would have put up with
these tiresome people at Corinth? Here they were, a
handful of men and women who had been so seized by
the gospel message that they had committed themselves
to the cause of Christ. But what poor advertisements
they were for their new-found faith – quarrelling among
themselves, turning the most holy celebration of the
Lord's death into a drunken debauch, and a spectacle of
unchristian behaviour which must have repelled enquir-
ing pagans from wanting to have anything more to do
with Christianity. Not the least of their failures was their
disloyalty to Paul himself, their heart-breaking readiness
to supplant him in favour of 'false apostles' who under-
mined his authority, discredited his motives and did their
best to blacken his reputation. That they should have
done all this when he was unable to defend himself, and
was burdened with the problems of the Ephesian
mission, is the mark of such fickleness as would have
made any ordinary missionary want to wash his hands
of them.

But this was just what Paul was not prepared to do.
In view of their record one cannot resist the feeling at
first that some of the flattering things Paul says about
the Corinthian church must have been said with tongue
in cheek. But it is a mark of Paul's greatness of spirit that
he obviously meant every word he wrote. However much
he deplored their behaviour, and took them to task for
it, he loved his black sheep in Corinth with the same
kind of love as Jesus felt for those who wronged him.
There is a divine quality of love in Paul's forgiveness
of his foolish and wayward flock, a power of tolerance
and understanding that only the greatest of the saints
have shown.

PAUL'S FIRST LETTER TO THE CORINTHIANS

1 From Paul, who by the will of God was called to be an apostle of Christ Jesus, and from our brother Sosthenes —

² To the church of God which is in Corinth, to all who are called to be God's people, who belong to him in union with Christ Jesus, together with all people everywhere who call on the name of our Lord Jesus Christ, their Lord and ours:

³ May God our Father and the Lord Jesus Christ give you grace and peace.

Blessings in Christ

⁴ I always give thanks to my God for you, because of the grace he has given you through Christ Jesus. ⁵ For in union with Christ you have become rich in all things, including all speech and all knowledge. ⁶ The message about Christ has become so firmly fixed in you, ⁷ that you have not failed to receive a single blessing, as you wait for our Lord Jesus Christ to be revealed. ⁸ He will also keep you firm to the end, so that you will be found without fault in the Day of our Lord Jesus Christ. ⁹ God is to be trusted, the God who called you to have fellowship with his Son Jesus Christ, our Lord.

Divisions in the Church

¹⁰ I appeal to you, brothers, by the authority of our Lord Jesus Christ: agree, all of you, in what you say, so there will be no divisions among you; be completely united, with only one thought and one purpose. ¹¹ For some people from Chloe's family have told me quite plainly, my brothers, that there are quarrels among you. ¹² Let me put it this way: each one of you says something different. One says, "I am with Paul"; another, "I am with Apollos"; another, "I am with Peter"; and another, "I am with Christ." ¹³ Christ has been split up into groups! Was it Paul who died on the cross for you? Were you baptized as Paul's disciples?

¹⁴ I thank God that I did not baptize any of you except Crispus and Gaius. ¹⁵ No one can say, then, that you were baptized as my disciples. ¹⁶ (Oh yes, I also baptized Steph-

anas and his family; but I can't remember whether I baptized anyone else.) 17 Christ did not send me to baptize. He sent me to tell the Good News, and to tell it without using the language of men's wisdom, for that would rob Christ's death on the cross of all its power.

Christ the Power and the Wisdom of God

18 For the message about Christ's death on the cross is nonsense to those who are being lost; but for us who are being saved, it is God's power. 19 For the scripture says,

"I will destroy the wisdom of the wise,
I will set aside the understanding of the scholars."

20 So then, where does that leave the wise men? Or the scholars? Or the skilful debaters of this world? God has shown that this world's wisdom is foolishness!

21 For God in his wisdom made it impossible for men to know him by means of their own wisdom. Instead, God decided to save those who believe, by means of the "foolish" message we preach. 22 Jews want miracles for proof, and Greeks look for wisdom. 23 As for us, we proclaim Christ on the cross, a message that is offensive to the Jews and nonsense to the Gentiles; 24 but for those whom God has called, both Jews and Gentiles, this message is Christ, who is the power of God and the wisdom of God. 25 For what seems to be God's foolishness is wiser than men's wisdom, and what seems to be God's weakness is stronger than men's strength.

26 Now remember what you were, brothers, when God

called you. Few of you were wise, or powerful, or of high social status, from the human point of view. [27] God purposely chose what the world considers nonsense in order to put wise men to shame, and what the world considers weak in order to put powerful men to shame. [28] He chose what the world looks down on, and despises, and thinks is nothing, in order to destroy what the world thinks is important. [29] This means that no single person can boast in God's presence. [30] But God has brought you into union with Christ Jesus, and God has made Christ to be our wisdom; by him we are put right with God, we become God's own people, and are set free. [31] Therefore, as the scripture says, "Whoever wants to boast must boast of what the Lord has done."

The Message about Christ on the Cross

2 When I came to you, my brothers, to preach God's secret truth to you, I did not use long words and great learning. [2] For I made up my mind to forget everything while I was with you except Jesus Christ, and especially

his death on the cross. [3] So when I came to you I was weak and trembled all over with fear, [4] and my speech and message were not delivered with skilful words of human wisdom, but with convincing proof of the power of

God's Spirit. ⁵ Your faith, then, does not rest on man's wisdom, but on God's power.

God's Wisdom

⁶ Yet I do speak wisdom to those who are spiritually mature. But it is not the wisdom that belongs to this world, or to the powers that rule this world — powers which are losing their power. ⁷ The wisdom I speak is God's secret wisdom, hidden from men, which God had already chosen for our glory, even before the world was made. ⁸ None of the rulers of this world knew this wisdom. If they had known it, they would not have nailed the Lord of glory to the cross. ⁹ However, as the scripture says,

> "What no man ever saw or heard,
> What no man ever thought could happen,
> Is the very thing God prepared for those
>   who love him."

¹⁰ But it was to us that God made known his secret, by means of his Spirit. The Spirit searches everything, even the hidden depths of God's purposes. ¹¹ As for a man, it is his own spirit within him that knows all about him; in the same way, only God's Spirit knows all about God. ¹² We have not received this world's spirit; we have received the Spirit sent by God, that we may know all that God has given us.

¹³ So then, we do not speak in words taught by human wisdom, but in words taught by the Spirit, as we explain spiritual truths to those who have the Spirit. ¹⁴ But the man who does not have the Spirit cannot receive the gifts that come from God's Spirit. He really does not understand them; they are nonsense to him, because their value can be judged only on a spiritual basis. ¹⁵ The man who has the Spirit is able to judge the value of everything, but no one is able to judge him. ¹⁶ As the scripture says,

> "Who knows the mind of the Lord?
> Who is able to give him advice?"

We, however, have the mind of Christ.

Servants of God

3 As a matter of fact, brothers, I could not talk to you as I talk to men who have the Spirit; I had to talk to you as men of this world, as children in the Christian

faith. ² I had to feed you milk, not solid food, because you were not ready for it. And even now you are not ready for it, ³ because you still live as men of this world. When there is jealousy among you, and you quarrel with one another, doesn't this prove that you are men of this world, living by this world's standards? ⁴ When one of you says, "I am with Paul," and another, "I am with Apollos" — aren't you acting like worldly men?

⁵ After all, who is Apollos? And who is Paul? We are simply God's servants, by whom you were led to believe. Each one of us does the work the Lord gave him to do:

⁶ I planted the seed, Apollos watered the plant, but it was God who made the plant grow. ⁷ The one who plants and the one who waters really do not matter. It is God who matters, for he makes the plant grow. ⁸ There is no difference between the man who plants and the man who waters; God will reward each one according to the work he has done. ⁹ For we are partners working together for God, and you are God's field.

You are also God's building. ¹⁰ Using the gift that God gave me, I did the work of an expert builder and laid the foundation, and another man is building upon it. But each one must be careful how he builds. ¹¹ For God has already placed Jesus Christ as the one and only foundation, and no other foundation can be laid. ¹² Some will use gold, or silver, or precious stones in building upon the foundation; others will use wood, or grass, or straw. ¹³ And the quality of each man's work will be seen when the Day of Christ exposes it. For that Day's fire will reveal every man's work: the fire will test it and show its real quality. 14 If what a man built on the foundation survives the fire, he will receive a reward. 15 But if any man's work is burnt up, then he will lose it; but he himself will be saved, as if he had escaped through the fire.

16 Surely you know that you are God's temple, and that God's Spirit lives in you! 17 So if anyone destroys God's temple, God will destroy him. For God's temple is holy, and you yourselves are his temple.

18 No one should fool himself. If anyone among you thinks that he is a wise man by this world's standards, he should become a fool, in order to be really wise. 19 For what this world considers to be wisdom is nonsense in God's sight. As the scripture says, "God traps the wise men in their cleverness"; 20 and another scripture says, "The Lord knows that the thoughts of the wise are worthless." 21 No one, then, should boast about what men can do. Actually everything belongs to you: 22 Paul, Apollos, and Peter; this world, life and death, the present and the future; all of these are yours, 23 and you belong to Christ, and Christ belongs to God.

Apostles of Christ

4 You should look on us as Christ's servants who have been put in charge of God's secret truths. 2 The one thing required of the man in charge is that he be faithful to his master. 3 Now, I am not at all concerned about being judged by you, or by any human standard; I don't even pass judgment on myself. 4 My conscience is clear, but that does not prove that I am really innocent. The Lord is the one who passes judgment on me. 5 So you should not pass judgment on anyone before the right time comes. Final judgment must wait until the Lord comes: he will bring to light the dark secrets and expose the hidden purposes of men's hearts. And then every man will receive from God the praise he deserves.

6 For your sake, brothers, I have applied all this to Apollos and me. I have used us as an example, that you may learn what the saying means, "Observe the proper rules." None of you should be proud of one man and despise the other. 7 Who made you superior to the others?

Didn't God give you everything you have? Well, then, how can you brag, as if what you have were not a gift?

8 Already you have everything you need! Already you are rich! You have become kings, even though we are not! Well, I wish you really were kings, so that we could be kings together with you. 9 For it seems to me that God has given us apostles the very last place, like men condemned to die in public, as a spectacle for the whole world of angels and of men. 10 For Christ's sake we are fools; but you are wise in Christ! We are weak, but you are strong! We are despised, but you are honoured! 11 To this very hour we go hungry and thirsty; we are clothed in rags; we are beaten; we wander from place to place; 12 we work hard to support ourselves. When we are cursed, we bless; when we are persecuted, we endure; 13 when we are insulted, we answer back with kind words. We are no more than this world's garbage; we are the scum of the earth to this very hour!

14 I write like this to you, not because I want to make you feel ashamed; I do it to instruct you as my own dear children. 15 For even if you have ten thousand teachers in your life in Christ, you have only one father. For in your life in Christ Jesus I have become your father, by bringing the Good News to you. 16 I beg you, then, follow my example. 17 For this purpose I am sending Timothy to you. He is my own dear and faithful son in the Lord. He will remind you of the principles which I follow in the new life in Christ Jesus, and which I teach in all the churches everywhere.

18 Some of you have become proud, thinking that I would not be coming to visit you. 19 If the Lord is willing, however, I will come to you soon, and then I will find out for myself what these proud ones can do, and not just what they can say! 20 For the Kingdom of God is not a matter of words, but of power. 21 Which do you prefer? Shall I come to you with a whip, or with a heart of love and gentleness?

Immorality in the Church

5 Now, it is actually being said that there is sexual immorality among you so terrible that not even the heathen would be guilty of it; for I am told that a man is living with his stepmother! 2 How then, can you be proud?

On the contrary, you should be filled with sadness, and the man who has done such a thing should be put out of your group! ³ As for me, even though I am far away from you in body, still I am there with you in spirit; and in the name of our Lord Jesus I have already passed judgment on the man who has done this terrible thing, as though I were there with you. ⁴ As you meet together, and I meet with you in my spirit, by the power of our Lord Jesus present with us, ⁵ you are to hand this man over to Satan for his body to be destroyed, so that his spirit may be saved in the Day of the Lord.

⁶ It is not right for you to be proud! You know the saying, "A little bit of yeast makes the whole batch of dough rise." ⁷ You must take out this old yeast of sin so that you will be entirely pure. Then you will be like a new batch of dough without any yeast, as indeed I know you actually are. For our Passover feast is ready, now that Christ, our Passover lamb, has been sacrificed. ⁸ Let us celebrate our feast, then, not with bread having the old yeast, the yeast of sin and immorality, but with the bread that has no yeast, the bread of purity and truth.

⁹ In the letter that I wrote you I told you not to associate with immoral people. ¹⁰ Now, I did not mean pagans who are immoral, or greedy, or lawbreakers, or who worship idols. To avoid them you would have to get out of the world completely! ¹¹ What I meant was that you should not associate with a man who calls himself a brother but is immoral, or greedy, or worships idols, or is a slanderer, or a drunkard, or a lawbreaker. Don't even sit down to eat with such a person.

¹²⁻¹³ After all, it is none of my business to judge outsiders. God will judge them. But should you not judge the members of your own fellowship? As the scripture says, "Take the evil man out of your group."

Lawsuits against Brothers

6 If one of you has a dispute with a brother, how dare he go before heathen judges, instead of letting God's people settle the matter? ² Don't you know that God's people will judge the world? Well, then, if you are to judge the world, aren't you capable of judging small matters? ³ Do you not know that we shall judge the angels? How much more, then, the things of this life! ⁴ If, then, such

matters come up, are you going to take them to be settled by people who have no standing in the church? [5] Shame on you! Surely there is at least one wise man in your fellowship who can settle a dispute between the brothers! [6] Instead, one brother goes to court against another, and lets unbelievers judge the case!

[7] The very fact that you have legal disputes among yourselves shows that you have failed completely. Would it not be better for you to be wronged? Would it not be better for you to be robbed? [8] Instead, you yourselves wrong one another, and rob one another, even your very brothers! [9] Surely you know that the wicked will not receive God's Kingdom. Do not fool yourselves: people who are immoral, or worship idols, or are adulterers, or homosexual perverts, [10] or who rob, or are greedy, or are drunkards, or who slander others, or are lawbreakers — none of these will receive God's Kingdom. [11] Some of you were like that. But you have been cleansed from sin; you have been dedicated to God; you have been put right with God through the name of the Lord Jesus Christ and by the Spirit of our God.

Use Your Bodies for God's Glory

[12] Someone will say, "I am allowed to do anything." Yes; but not everything is good for you. I could say, "I am allowed to do anything"; but I am not going to let anything make a slave of me. [13] Someone else will say, "Food is for the stomach, and the stomach is for food." Yes; but God will put an end to both. A man's body is not meant for immorality, but for the Lord; and the Lord is for the body. [14] God raised the Lord from death, and he will also raise us by his power.

[15] You know that your bodies are parts of the body of Christ. Shall I take a part of Christ's body and make it part of the body of a prostitute? Impossible! [16] Or perhaps you don't know that the man who joins his body to a prostitute becomes physically one with her? The scripture says quite plainly, "The two will become one body." [17] But he who joins himself to the Lord becomes spiritually one with him.

[18] Avoid immorality. Any other sin a man commits does not affect his body; but the man who commits immorality sins against his own body. [19] Don't you know that your

body is the temple of the Holy Spirit, who lives in you, the Spirit given you by God? You do not belong to yourselves but to God; 20 he bought you for a price. So use your bodies for God's glory.

Questions about Marriage

7 Now, to deal with the matters you wrote about. A man does well not to marry. 2 But because there is so much immorality, every man should have his own wife, and every woman should have her own husband. 8 A man should fulfil his duty as a husband and a woman should fulfil her duty as a wife, and each should satisfy the other's needs. 4 The wife is not the master of her own body, but the husband is; in the same way the husband is not the master of his own body, but the wife is. 5 Do not deny yourselves to each other, unless you first agree to do so for a while, in order to spend your time in prayer; but then resume normal marital relations, so that your lack of self-control will not make you give in to Satan's temptation.

6 I tell you this not as an order, but simply as a permission. 7 Actually I would prefer that all were as I am; but each one has the special gift that God has given him, one man this gift, another man that.

8 Now, I say this to the unmarried and to the widows: it would be better for you to continue to live alone, as I do. 9 But if you cannot restrain your desires, go on and marry — it is better to marry than to burn with passion.

10 For married people I have a command, not my own but the Lord's: a married woman must not leave her husband; 11 if she does, she must remain single or else be reconciled to her husband; and a husband must not divorce his wife.

12 To the others I say (I, myself, not the Lord): if a Christian man has a wife who is an unbeliever and she agrees to go on living with him, he must not divorce her. 13 And if a Christian woman is married to a man who is an unbeliever, and he agrees to go on living with her, she must not divorce him. 14 For the unbelieving husband is made acceptable to God by being united to his wife, and the unbelieving wife is made acceptable to God by being united to her Christian husband. If this were not so, their children would be like pagan children; but as it is, they are acceptable to God. 15 However, if the one who is not

a believer wishes to leave the Christian partner, let him do so. In such cases the Christian partner, whether husband or wife, is free to choose; for God has called you to live in peace. ¹⁶ How can you be sure, Christian wife, that you will not save your husband? Or how can you be sure, Christian husband, that you will not save your wife?

Live as God Called You

¹⁷ Each one should go on living according to the Lord's gift to him, and as he was when God called him. This is the rule I teach in all the churches. ¹⁸ If a circumcised man has accepted God's call, he should not try to remove the marks of circumcision; if an uncircumcised man has accepted God's call, he should not get circumcised. ¹⁹ Because being circumcised or not means nothing. What matters is to obey God's commandments. ²⁰ Every man should remain as he was when he accepted God's call. ²¹ Were you a slave when God called you? Well, never mind; but if you do have a chance to become a free man, use it. ²² For a slave who has been called by the Lord is the Lord's free man; in the same way a free man who has been called by Christ is his slave. ²³ God bought you for a price; so do not become men's slaves. ²⁴ Brothers, each one should remain in fellowship with God as he was when he was called.

Questions about the Unmarried and the Widows

²⁵ Now, the matter about the unmarried: I do not have a command from the Lord, but I give my opinion as one who by the Lord's mercy is worthy of trust.

²⁶ Considering the present distress, I think it is better for a man to stay as he is. ²⁷ Do you have a wife? Then don't try to get rid of her. Are you unmarried? Then don't look for a wife. ²⁸ But if you do marry, you haven't committed a sin; and if an unmarried woman marries, she hasn't committed a sin. But I would rather spare you the everyday troubles that such people will have.

²⁹ This is what I mean, brothers: there is not much time left, and from now on married men should live as though they were not married; ³⁰ those who weep, as though they were not sad; those who laugh, as though they were not happy; those who buy, as though they did not own what they bought; ³¹ those who deal in worldly goods, as though

they were not fully occupied with them. For this world, as it is now, will not last much longer.

³² I would like you to be free from worry. An unmarried man concerns himself with the Lord's work, because he is trying to please the Lord; ³³ but a married man concerns himself with worldly matters, because he wants to please his wife, ³⁴ and so he is pulled in two directions. An unmarried woman or a virgin concerns herself with the Lord's work, because she wants to be dedicated both in body and spirit; but a married woman concerns herself with worldly matters, because she wants to please her husband.

³⁵ I am saying this because I want to help you. I am not trying to put restrictions on you. Instead, I want you to do what is right and proper, and give yourselves completely to the Lord's service without any reservation.

³⁶ In the case of an engaged couple who have decided not to marry: if the man feels that he is not acting properly toward the girl; if his passions are too strong, and he feels that they ought to marry, then they should get married, as he wants to. There is no sin in this. ³⁷ But if a man, without being forced to do so, has firmly made up his mind not to marry; if he has his will under complete control, and has already decided in his own mind what to do — then he does well not to marry the girl. ³⁸ So the man who marries his girl does well, but the one who does not marry her will do even better.

³⁹ A married woman is not free as long as her husband lives; but if her husband dies, then she is free to be married to the man she wants; but it must be a Christian marriage. ⁴⁰ She will be happier, however, if she stays as she is. That is my opinion, and I think that I too have God's Spirit.

The Question about Food Offered to Idols

8 Now, the matter about food offered to idols.
It is true, of course, that "all of us have knowledge," as they say. Such knowledge, however, puffs a man up with pride; but love builds up. ² The person who thinks he knows something really doesn't know as he ought to know. ³ But the man who loves God is known by him.

⁴ So then, about eating the food offered to idols: we know that an idol stands for something that does not really

exist; we know that there is only the one God. [5] Even if there are so-called "gods," whether in heaven or on earth, and even though there are many of these "gods" and "lords," [6] yet there is for us only one God, the Father, who is the creator of all things, and for whom we live; and there is only one Lord, Jesus Christ, through whom all things were created, and through whom we live.

[7] But not everyone knows this truth. Certain people are so used to idols that to this very day when they eat such food they still think of it as food that belongs to an idol; their conscience is weak and they feel they are defiled by the food. [8] Food, however, will not bring us any closer to God; we shall not lose anything if we do not eat, nor shall we gain anything if we do eat.

[9] Be careful, however, and do not let your freedom of action make those who are weak in the faith fall into sin. [10] For if a man whose conscience is weak in this matter sees you, who have "knowledge," eating in the temple of an idol, will not this encourage him to eat food offered to idols? [11] And so this weak man, your brother for whom Christ died, will perish because of your "knowledge"! [12] And in this way you will be sinning against Christ by sinning against your brothers and wounding their weak conscience. [13] If food makes my brother sin, I myself will never eat meat again, so as not to make my brother fall into sin.

Rights and Duties of an Apostle

9 Am I not a free man? Am I not an apostle? Haven't I seen Jesus our Lord? And aren't you the result of my work for the Lord? [2] Even if others do not accept me

as an apostle, surely you do! You yourselves, because of your life in the Lord, are proof of the fact that I am an apostle.

⁸ When people criticize me, this is how I defend myself: ⁴ Don't I have the right to be given food and drink for my work? ⁵ Don't I have the right to do what the other apostles do, and the Lord's brothers, and Peter, and take a Christian wife with me on my trips? ⁶ Or are Barnabas and I the only ones who have to work for our living? ⁷ Who ever heard of a soldier who paid his own expenses in the army? Or of a farmer who did not eat the grapes from his own vineyard? Or of a shepherd who did not use the milk from his own sheep?

⁸ I don't have to limit myself to these everyday examples, for the Law says the same thing. ⁹ We read in the Law of Moses, "Do not tie up the mouth of the ox when it treads out the grain." Now, is God concerned about oxen? ¹⁰ Or did he not really mean us when he said this? Of course this was written for us! The man who plows and the man who reaps should do their work in the hope of getting a share of the crop. ¹¹ We have sown spiritual seed among you. Is it too much if we reap material benefits from you? ¹² If others have the right to expect this from you, don't we have an even greater right?

But we haven't made use of this right. Instead, we have endured everything in order not to put any obstacle in the way of the Good News about Christ. ¹³ Surely you know that the men who work in the Temple get their food from the Temple, and that those who offer the sacrifices on the altar get a share of the sacrifices. ¹⁴ In the same way, the Lord has ordered that those who preach the gospel should get their living from it.

¹⁵ But I haven't made use of any of these rights, nor am I writing this now in order to claim such rights for myself. I would rather die first! Nobody is going to turn my rightful boast into empty words! ¹⁶ I have no right to boast just because I preach the gospel. After all, I am under orders to do so. And how terrible it would be for me if I did not preach the gospel! ¹⁷ If I did my work as a matter of free choice, then I could expect to be paid; but since I do it as a matter of duty, it means that I do it as a job given me to do. ¹⁸ What pay do I get, then? It is the privilege of preaching the Good News without charging

for it, without claiming my rights in my work for the gospel.

¹⁹ I am a free man, nobody's slave; but I make myself everybody's slave in order to win as many as possible. ²⁰ While working with the Jews, I live like a Jew in order to win them; and even though I myself am not subject to the Law of Moses, I live as though I were, when working with those who are, in order to win them. ²¹ In the same way, when with Gentiles I live like a Gentile, outside the Jewish Law, in order to win Gentiles. This does not mean that I don't obey God's law, for I am really under Christ's law. ²² Among the weak in faith I become weak like one of them, in order to win them. So I become all things to all men, that I may save some of them by any means possible.

²³ All this I do for the gospel's sake, in order to share in its blessings. ²⁴ Surely you know that in a race all the runners take part in it, but only one of them wins the prize.

Run, then, in such a way as to win the prize. ²⁵ Every athlete in training submits to strict discipline; he does so in order to be crowned with a wreath that will not last; but we do it for one that will last for ever. ²⁶ That is why I run straight for the finish line; that is why I am like a boxer, who does not waste his punches. ²⁷ I harden my body with blows and bring it under complete control, to keep from being rejected myself after having called others to the contest.

Warning against Idols

10 I want you to remember, brothers, what happened to our ancestors who followed Moses. They were all under the protection of the cloud, and all passed safely

through the Red Sea. ² In the cloud and in the sea they were all baptized as followers of Moses. ³ All ate the same spiritual bread, ⁴ and all drank the same spiritual drink; for they drank from that spiritual rock that went along with them; and that rock was Christ himself. ⁵ But even then God was not pleased with most of them, and so their dead bodies were scattered over the desert.

⁶ Now, all these things are examples for us, to warn us not to desire evil things, as they did, ⁷ nor to worship idols, as some of them did. As the scripture says, "The people sat down to eat and drink, and got up to dance." ⁸ We must not commit sexual immorality, as some of them did — and in one day twenty-three thousand of them fell dead. ⁹ We must not put the Lord to the test, as some of them did — and they were killed by the snakes. ¹⁰ You must not complain, as some of them did — and they were destroyed by the Angel of Death.

¹¹ All these things happened to them as examples for others, and they were written down as a warning for us. For we live at the time when the end is about to come.

¹² The one who thinks he is standing up had better be careful that he does not fall. ¹³ Every temptation that has come your way is the kind that normally comes to people.

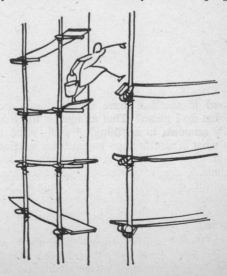

For God keeps his promise, and he will not allow you to be tempted beyond your power to resist; but at the time you are tempted he will give you the strength to endure it, and so provide you with a way out.

¹⁴ So then, my dear friends, keep away from the worship of idols. ¹⁵ I speak to you as sensible people; judge for yourselves what I say. ¹⁶ The cup of blessing for which we give thanks to God: do we not share in the blood of Christ when we drink from this cup? And the bread we break: do we not share in the body of Christ when we eat this bread? ¹⁷ Because there is the one bread, all of us, though many, are one body; for we all share the same loaf.

¹⁸ Consider the Hebrew people: those who eat what is offered in sacrifice share in the altar's service to God. ¹⁹ What do I mean? That an idol or the food offered to it really amounts to anything? ²⁰ No! What I am saying is that what is sacrificed on pagan altars is offered to demons, not to God. And I do not want you to be partners with demons. ²¹ You cannot drink from the Lord's cup and also from the cup of demons; you cannot eat at the Lord's table and also at the table of demons. ²² Or do we want to make the Lord jealous? Do you think that we are stronger than he?

²³ "We are allowed to do anything," so they say. Yes, but not everything is good. "We are allowed to do anything" — but not everything is helpful. ²⁴ No one should

be looking out for his own interests, but for the interests of others.

25 You are free to eat anything sold in the meat market, without asking any questions because of conscience. 26 For, as the scripture says, "The earth and everything in it belong to the Lord."

27 If an unbeliever invites you to a meal and you decide to go, eat what is set before you without asking any questions because of conscience. 28 But if someone tells you, "This is food that was offered to idols," then do not eat that food, for the sake of the one who told you so and for conscience' sake — 29 that is, not your own conscience, but the other man's conscience.

"Well, then," someone asks, "why should my freedom to act be limited by another person's conscience? 30 If I thank God for my food, why should anyone criticize me about food for which I give thanks?"

31 Well, whatever you do, whether you eat or drink, do it all for God's glory. 32 Live in such a way as to cause no trouble either to Jews, or Gentiles, or to the church of God. 33 Just do as I do: I try to please everyone in all that I do, with no thought of my own good, but for the good of all, so they might be saved.

11 Imitate me, then, just as I imitate Christ.

Covering the Head in Worship

2 I do praise you because you always remember me and follow the teachings that I have handed on to you. 3 But I want you to understand that Christ is supreme over every man, the husband is supreme over his wife, and God is supreme over Christ. 4 So a man who in public worship prays or speaks God's message with his head covered disgraces Christ. 5 And any woman who in public worship prays or speaks God's message with nothing on her head disgraces her husband; there is no difference between her and a woman whose head has been shaved. 6 If the woman does not cover her head, she might as well cut her hair. And since it is a shameful thing for a woman to shave her head or cut her hair, she should cover her head. 7 A man has no need to cover his head, because he reflects the image and glory of God. But woman reflects the glory of man; 8 for man was not created from woman, but woman from

man. [9] Nor was man created for woman's sake, but woman was created for man's sake. [10] On account of the angels, then, a woman should have a covering over her head to show that she is under her husband's authority. [11] In our life in the Lord, however, woman is not independent of man, nor is man independent of woman. [12] For as woman was made from man, in the same way man is born of woman; and all things come from God.

[13] Judge for yourselves: is it proper for a woman to pray to God in public worship with nothing on her head? [14] Why, nature herself teaches you that long hair is a disgraceful thing for a man, [15] but is a woman's pride. Her long hair has been given her to serve as a covering. [16] But if anyone wants to argue about it, all I have to say is that neither we nor the churches of God have any other custom in worship.

The Lord's Supper

[17] In the following instructions, however, I do not praise you; for your church meetings actually do more harm than good. [18] In the first place, I have been told that there are opposing groups in your church meetings; and this I believe is partly true. [19] (No doubt there must be divisions among you so that the ones who are in the right may be clearly seen.) [20] When you meet together as a group, you do not come to eat the Lord's Supper. [21] For as you eat, each one goes ahead with his own meal, so that some are hungry while others get drunk. [22] Don't you have your own homes in which to eat and drink? Or would you rather despise the church of God and put to shame the people who are in need? What do you expect me to say to you about this? Should I praise you? Of course I do not praise you!

[23] For from the Lord I received the teaching that I passed on to you: that the Lord Jesus, on the night he was betrayed, took the bread, [24] gave thanks to God, broke it, and said, "This is my body, which is for you. Do this in memory of me." [25] In the same way, he took the cup after the supper and said, "This cup is God's new covenant, sealed with my blood. Whenever you drink it, do it in memory of me." [26] For until the Lord comes, you proclaim his death whenever you eat this bread and drink from this cup.

²⁷ It follows, then, that if anyone eats the Lord's bread or drinks from his cup in an improper manner, he is guilty of sin against the Lord's body and blood. ²⁸ Everyone should examine himself, therefore, and with this attitude eat the bread and drink from the cup. ²⁹ For if he does not recognize the meaning of the Lord's body when he eats the bread and drinks from the cup, he brings judgment on himself as he eats and drinks. ³⁰ That is why many of you are sick and weak, and several have died. ³¹ If we would examine ourselves first, we would not come under God's judgment. ³² But we are judged and punished by the Lord, so that we shall not be condemned along with the world.

³³ So then, my brothers, when you gather together to eat the Lord's meal, wait for one another. ³⁴ And if anyone is hungry, he should eat at home, so that you will not come under God's judgment as you meet together. As for the other matters, I will settle them when I come.

Gifts from the Holy Spirit

12 Now, the matter about the gifts from the Holy Spirit.

I want you to know the truth about them, my brothers. ² You know that while you were still heathen you were controlled by dead idols, who always led you astray. ³ You must realize, then, that no one who is led by God's Spirit can say, "A curse on Jesus!", and no one can confess "Jesus is Lord," unless he is guided by the Holy Spirit.

⁴ There are different kinds of spiritual gifts, but the same Spirit gives them. ⁵ There are different ways of serving, but the same Lord is served. ⁶ There are different abilities to perform service, but the same God gives ability to everyone for all services. ⁷ Each one is given some proof of the Spirit's presence for the good of all. ⁸ The Spirit gives one man a message of wisdom, while to another man the same Spirit gives a message of knowledge. ⁹ One and the same Spirit gives faith to one man, while to another man he gives the power to heal. ¹⁰ The Spirit gives one man the power to work miracles; to another, the gift of speaking God's message; and to yet another, the ability to tell the difference between gifts that come from the Spirit and those that do not. To one man he gives the ability to speak with strange sounds; to

another, he gives the ability to explain what these sounds mean. ¹¹ But it is one and the same Spirit who does all this; he gives a different gift to each man, as he wishes.

One Body with Many Parts

¹² For Christ is like a single body, which has many parts; it is still one body, even though it is made up of different parts. ¹³ In the same way, all of us, Jews and Gentiles, slaves and free men, have been baptized into the one body by the same Spirit, and we have all been given the one Spirit to drink.

¹⁴ For the body itself is not made up of only one part, but of many parts. ¹⁵ If the foot were to say, "Because I am not a hand, I don't belong to the body," that would not make it stop being a part of the body. ¹⁶ And if the ear were to say, "Because I am not an eye, I don't belong to the body," that would not make it stop being a part of the body. ¹⁷ If the whole body were just an eye, how could it hear? And if it were only an ear, how could it smell? ¹⁸ As it is, however, God put every different part in the body just as he wished. ¹⁹ There would not be a body if it were all only one part! ²⁰ As it is, there are many parts, and one body.

²¹ So then, the eye cannot say to the hand, "I don't need you!" Nor can the head say to the feet, "Well, I don't need you!" ²² On the contrary; we cannot get along without the parts of the body that seem to be weaker, ²³ and those parts that we think aren't worth very much are the ones which we treat with greater care; while the parts of the body which don't look very nice receive special attention, ²⁴ which the more beautiful parts of our body do not need. God himself has put our bodies together in such a way as to give greater honour to those parts that lack it. ²⁵ And so there is no division in the body, but all its different parts have the same concern for one another. ²⁶ If one part of the body suffers, all the other parts suffer with it; if one part is praised, all the other parts share its happiness.

²⁷ All of you, then, are Christ's body, and each one is a part of it. ²⁸ In the church, then, God has put all in place: in the first place, apostles, in the second place, prophets, and in the third place, teachers; then those who perform miracles, followed by those who are given the power to heal, or to help others, or to direct them, or to speak with

strange sounds. [29] They are not all apostles, or prophets, or teachers. Not all have the power to work miracles, [30] or to heal diseases, or to speak with strange sounds, or to explain what these sounds mean. [31] Set your hearts, then, on the more important gifts.

Best of all, however, is the following way.

Love

13 I may be able to speak the languages of men and even of angels, but if I have not love, my speech is no more than a noisy gong or a clanging bell. [2] I may have the gift of inspired preaching; I may have all knowledge and understand all secrets; I may have all the faith needed to move mountains — but if I have not love, I am nothing. [3] I may give away everything I have, and even give up my body to be burned — but if I have not love, it does me no good.

[4] Love is patient and kind; love is not jealous, or conceited, or proud; [5] love is not ill-mannered, or selfish, or irritable; love does not keep a record of wrongs; [6] love is not happy with evil, but is happy with the truth. [7] Love never gives up: its faith, hope, and patience never fail.

[8] Love is eternal. There are inspired messages, but they are temporary; there are gifts of speaking, but they will cease; there is knowledge, but it will pass. [9] For our gifts of knowledge and of inspired messages are only partial; [10] but when what is perfect comes, then what is partial will disappear.

[11] When I was a child, my speech, feelings, and thinking were all those of a child; now that I am a man, I have no more use for childish ways. [12] What we see now is like

the dim image in a mirror; then we shall see face to face. What I know now is only partial; then it will be complete, as complete as God's knowledge of me.

¹³ Meanwhile these three remain: faith, hope, and love; and the greatest of these is love.

More about Gifts from the Spirit

14 It is love, then, that you should strive for. Set your hearts on spiritual gifts, especially the gift of speaking God's message. ² The one who speaks with strange sounds does not speak to men but to God, because no one understands him. He is speaking secret truths by the power of the Spirit. ³ But the one who speaks God's message speaks to men, and gives them help, encouragement, and comfort. ⁴ The man who speaks with strange sounds helps only himself, but the one who speaks God's message helps the whole church.

⁵ I would like for all of you to speak with strange sounds; but I would rather that all of you had the gift of speaking God's message. For the man who speaks God's message is of greater value than the one who speaks with strange sounds — unless there is someone present who can explain what he says, so that the whole church may be helped. ⁶ So when I come to you, brothers, what use will I be to you if I speak with strange sounds? Not a bit, unless I bring you some revelation from God, or some knowledge, or some inspired message or teaching.

⁷ Even such lifeless musical instruments as the flute and the harp — how will anyone know the tune that is being played unless the notes are sounded distinctly? ⁸ And if the man who plays the bugle does not sound a clear call, who will prepare for battle? ⁹ In the same way, how will anyone understand what you are talking about if your message by means of strange sounds is not clear? Your words will vanish in the air! ¹⁰ There are many different languages in the world, yet not a single one of them is without meaning. ¹¹ But if I do not know the language being spoken, the man who uses it will be a foreigner to me and I will be a foreigner to him. ¹² Since you are eager to have the gifts of the Spirit, above everything else you must try to make greater use of those which help build up the church.

¹³ The man who speaks with strange sounds, then, must

pray for the gift to explain what they mean. ¹⁴ For if I pray in this way, my spirit prays indeed, but my mind has no part in it. ¹⁵ What should I do, then? I will pray with my spirit, but I will pray also with my mind; I will sing with my spirit, but I will sing also with my mind. ¹⁶ When you give thanks to God in spirit only, how can an ordinary man taking part in the meeting say "Amen" to your prayer of thanksgiving? He has no way of knowing what you are saying. ¹⁷ Even if your prayer of thanks to God is quite good, the other man is not helped at all.

¹⁸ I thank God that I speak with strange sounds much more than any of you. ¹⁹ But in church worship I would rather speak five words that can be understood, in order to teach others, than speak thousands of words with strange sounds.

²⁰ Do not be like children in your thinking, brothers; be children so far as evil is concerned, but be mature in your thinking. ²¹ In the Scriptures it is written:

"I will speak to this people, says the Lord:
I will speak through men of foreign languages,
And through the lips of foreigners.
But even then my people will not listen to me."

²² So then, the gift of speaking with strange sounds is proof for unbelievers, not for believers, while the gift of speaking God's message is proof for believers, not for unbelievers.

²³ If, then, the whole church meets together and everyone starts speaking with strange sounds — if some ordinary people or unbelievers come in, won't they say that you are all crazy? ²⁴ But if all speak God's message, when some unbeliever or ordinary person comes in he will be convinced of his sin by what he hears. He will be judged by all he hears, ²⁵ his secret thoughts will be brought into the open, and he will bow down and worship God, confessing, "Truly God is here with you!"

Order in the Church

²⁶ What do I mean, my brothers? When you meet for worship, one man has a hymn, another a teaching, another a revelation from God, another a message with strange sounds, and still another the explanation of what it means. Everything must be of help to the church. ²⁷ If someone is going to speak with strange sounds, two or three at the

most should speak, one after the other, and someone else must explain what is being said. 28 If no person is there who can explain, then no one should speak out in the meeting, but only to himself and to God. 29 Two or three who are given God's message should speak, while the others judge what they say. 30 But if someone sitting in the meeting receives a message from God, the one who is speaking should stop. 31 All of you may speak God's message, one by one, so that all will learn and be encouraged. 32 The gift of speaking God's message should be under the speaker's control; 33 for God has not called us to be disorderly, but peaceful.

As in all the churches of God's people, 34 the women should keep quiet in the church meetings. They are not allowed to speak; as the Jewish Law says, they must not be in charge. 35 If they want to find out about something, they should ask their husbands at home. It is a disgraceful thing for a woman to speak in a church meeting.

36 Or could it be that the word of God came from you? Or are you the only ones to whom it came? 37 If anyone supposes he is God's messenger or has a spiritual gift, he must realize that what I am writing you is the Lord's command. 38 But if he does not pay attention to this, pay no attention to him.

39 So then, my brothers, set your heart on speaking God's message, but do not forbid the speaking with strange sounds. 40 Everything must be done in a proper and orderly way.

The Resurrection of Christ

15 And now I want to remind you, brothers, of the Good News which I preached to you, which you received, and on which your faith stands firm. 2 That is the gospel, the message that I preached to you. You are saved by the gospel if you hold firmly to it — unless it was for nothing that you believed.

3 I passed on to you what I received, which is of the greatest importance: that Christ died for our sins, as written in the Scriptures; 4 that he was buried and raised to life on the third day, as written in the Scriptures; 5 that he appeared to Peter, and then to all twelve apostles. 6 Then he appeared to more than five hundred of his followers at once, most of whom are still alive, although

some have died. ⁷ Then he appeared to James, and then to all the apostles.

⁸ Last of all he appeared also to me — even though I am like one who was born in a most unusual way. ⁹ For I am the least of all the apostles — I do not even deserve to be called an apostle, because I persecuted God's church. ¹⁰ But by God's grace I am what I am, and the grace that he gave me was not without effect. On the contrary, I have worked harder than all the other apostles, although it was not really my own doing, but God's grace working with me. ¹¹ So then, whether it came from me or from them, this is what we all preach, this is what you believe.

Our Resurrection

¹² Now, since our message is that Christ has been raised from death, how can some of you say that the dead will not be raised to life? ¹³ If that is true, it means that Christ was not raised; ¹⁴ and if Christ has not been raised from death, then we have nothing to preach, and you have nothing to believe. ¹⁵ More than that, we are shown to be lying against God, because we said of him that he raised Christ from death — but he did not raise him, if it is true that the dead are not raised to life. ¹⁶ For if the dead are not raised, neither has Christ been raised. ¹⁷ And if Christ has not been raised, then your faith is a delusion and you are still lost in your sins. ¹⁸ It would also mean that the believers in Christ who have died are lost. ¹⁹ If our hope in Christ is good for this life only, and no more, then we deserve more pity than anyone else in all the world.

²⁰ But the truth is that Christ has been raised from death, as the guarantee that those who sleep in death will also be raised. ²¹ For just as death came by means of a man, in the same way the rising from death comes by means of a man. ²² For just as all men die because of their union to Adam, in the same way all will be raised to life because of their union to Christ. ²³ But each one in his proper order: Christ, the first of all; then those who belong to Christ, at the time of his coming. ²⁴ Then the end will come; Christ will overcome all spiritual rulers, authorities, and powers, and hand over the Kingdom to God the Father. ²⁵ For Christ must rule until God defeats all enemies and puts them under his feet. ²⁶ The last enemy to be defeated will be death. ²⁷ For the scripture says, "God put *all* things under his feet." It is clear, of course, that the words "all things" do not include God himself, who puts all things under Christ. ²⁸ But when all things have been placed under Christ's rule, then he himself, the Son, will place himself under God, who placed all under him; and God will rule completely over all.

²⁹ Now, what of those people who are baptized for the dead? What do they hope to accomplish? If it is true, as they claim, that the dead are not raised to life, why are they being baptized for the dead? ³⁰ And as for us — why would we run the risk of danger every hour? ³¹ Brothers, I face death every day! The pride I have in you in our life in Christ Jesus our Lord makes me declare this. ³² If, as it were, I have fought "wild beasts" here in Ephesus, simply from human motives, what have I gained? As the saying goes, "Let us eat and drink, for tomorrow we will die" — if the dead are not raised to life.

³³ Do not be fooled: "Bad companions ruin good character." ³⁴ Come back to your right senses and stop your sinful ways. I say this to your shame: some of you do not know God.

The Resurrection Body

³⁵ Someone will ask, "How can the dead be raised to life? What kind of body will they have?" ³⁶ You fool! When you plant a seed in the ground it does not sprout to life unless it dies. ³⁷ And what you plant in the ground is a bare seed, perhaps a grain of wheat, or of some other kind, not the full-bodied plant that will grow up. ³⁸ God

provides that seed with the body he wishes; he gives each seed its own proper body.

³⁹ And the flesh of living beings is not all the same kind of flesh: men have one kind of flesh, animals another, birds another, and fish another.

⁴⁰ And there are heavenly bodies and earthly bodies; there is a beauty that belongs to heavenly bodies, and another kind of beauty that belongs to earthly bodies. ⁴¹ The sun has its own beauty, the moon another beauty, and the stars a different beauty; and even among stars there are different kinds of beauty.

⁴² This is how it will be when the dead are raised to life. When the body is buried it is mortal; when raised, it will be immortal. ⁴³ When buried, it is ugly and weak; when raised, it will be beautiful and strong. ⁴⁴ When buried, it is a physical body; when raised, it will be a spiritual body. There is, of course, a physical body, so there has to be a spiritual body. ⁴⁵ For the scripture says: "The first man, Adam, was created a living being"; but the last Adam is the life-giving Spirit. ⁴⁶ It is not the spiritual that comes first, but the physical, and then the spiritual. ⁴⁷ The first Adam was made of the dust of the earth; the second Adam came from heaven. ⁴⁸ Those who belong to the earth are like the one who was made of earth; those who are of heaven are like the one who came from heaven. ⁴⁹ Just as we wear the likeness of the man made of earth, so we will wear the likeness of the Man from heaven.

⁵⁰ This is what I mean, brothers: what is made of flesh and blood cannot share in God's Kingdom, and what is mortal cannot possess immortality.

⁵¹ Listen to this secret: we shall not all die, but in an instant we shall all be changed, ⁵² as quickly as the blinking of an eye, when the last trumpet sounds. For when it sounds, the dead will be raised immortal beings, and we shall all be changed. ⁵³ For what is mortal must clothe itself with what is immortal; what will die must clothe itself with what cannot die. ⁵⁴ So when what is mortal has been clothed with what is immortal, and when what will die has been clothed with what cannot die, then the scripture will come true: "Death is destroyed; victory is complete!"

⁵⁵ "Where, O Death, is your victory?
Where, O Death, is your power to hurt?"

⁵⁶ Death gets its power to hurt from sin, and sin gets its power from the Law. ⁵⁷ But thanks be to God who gives us the victory through our Lord Jesus Christ!

⁵⁸ So then, my dear brothers, stand firm and steady. Keep busy always in your work for the Lord, since you know that nothing you do in the Lord's service is ever without value.

The Offering for Fellow Believers

16 Now the matter about the money to be raised to help God's people in Judea: you must do what I told the churches in Galatia to do. ² On the first day of every week each of you must put aside some money, in

proportion to what he has earned, and save it up, so there will be no need to collect money when I come. ³ After I come I shall send the men you have approved, with letters of introduction, to take your gift to Jerusalem. ⁴ If it seems worth while for me to go, then they will go along with me.

Paul's Plans

⁵ I shall come to you after I have gone through Macedonia — for I am going through Macedonia. ⁶ I shall probably spend some time with you, perhaps the whole

winter, and then you can help me to continue my trip,
wherever it is I shall go next. ⁷ For I do not want to see
you just briefly in passing. I hope to spend quite a long
time with you, if the Lord allows.

⁸ But I plan to stay here in Ephesus until the day of
Pentecost. ⁹ There is a real opportunity here for great and
worth-while work, even though there are many opponents.

¹⁰ If Timothy comes your way, however, be sure to
make him feel welcome among you, for he is working for
the Lord, just as I am. ¹¹ No one is to look down on him,
but you must help him continue his trip in peace, so that
he will come back to me; for I am expecting him back
with the brothers.

¹² Now, about brother Apollos: I have often encouraged him to visit you with the other brothers, but he is
not completely convinced that he should go right now.
When he gets the chance, however, he will go.

Final Words

¹³ Be alert, stand firm in the faith, be brave, be strong.
¹⁴ Do all your work in love.

¹⁵ You know about Stephanas and his family; they are
the first Christian converts in Greece, and have given
themselves to the service of God's people. I beg you, my
brothers, ¹⁶ to follow the leadership of such people as
these, and of anyone else who works and serves with them.

¹⁷ I am happy over the coming of Stephanas, Fortunatus,
and Achaicus; they have made up for your absence, ¹⁸ and
have cheered me up, just as they cheered you up. Such
men as these deserve notice.

¹⁹ The churches in the province of Asia send you their
greetings; Aquila and Priscilla and the church that meets
in their house send warm Christian greetings. ²⁰ All the
brothers here send greetings.

Greet one another with a brotherly kiss.

²¹ With my own hand I write this: *Greetings from
Paul.*

²² Whoever does not love the Lord — a curse on him!
Marana tha — Our Lord, come!

²³ The grace of the Lord Jesus be with you.

²⁴ My love be with you all in Christ Jesus.

PAUL'S SECOND LETTER TO THE CORINTHIANS

1 From Paul, apostle of Christ Jesus by God's will, and from our brother Timothy —

To the church of God in Corinth, and to all God's people in all Greece:

² May God our Father and the Lord Jesus Christ give you grace and peace.

Paul Gives Thanks to God

³ Let us give thanks to the God and Father of our Lord Jesus Christ, the merciful Father, the God from whom all help comes! ⁴ He helps us in all our troubles, so that we are able to help those who have all kinds of troubles, using the same help that we ourselves have received from God. ⁵ Just as we have a share in Christ's many sufferings, so also through Christ we share in his great help. ⁶ If we suffer, it is for your help and salvation; if we are helped, then you too are helped and given the strength to endure with patience the same sufferings that we also endure. ⁷ So our hope in you is never shaken; we know that just as you share in our sufferings, you also share in the help we receive.

⁸ For we want to remind you, brothers, of the trouble we had in the province of Asia. The burdens laid upon us were so great and so heavy, that we gave up all hope of living. ⁹ We felt that the sentence of death had been passed against us. But this happened so that we should rely, not upon ourselves, but only on God, who raises the dead. ¹⁰ From such terrible dangers of death he saved us, and will save us; and we have placed our hope in him that

he will save us again, [11] as you help us by means of your prayers for us. So it will be that the many prayers for us will be answered, and God will bless us; and many will raise their voices to him in thanksgiving for us.

The Change in Paul's Plans

[12] This is the thing we are proud of: our conscience assures us that our lives in this world, and especially our relations with you, have been ruled by God-given frankness and sincerity, by the power of God's grace, and not by human wisdom. [13] For we write to you only what you can read and understand. And I hope you will come to understand completely [14] what you now understand only in part, that in the Day of the Lord Jesus you can be as proud of us as we shall be of you.

[15] I was so sure of all this that I made plans at first to visit you in order that you might be blessed twice. [16] For I planned to visit you on my way to Macedonia and again on my way back, to get help from you for my trip to Judea. [17] In planning this did I appear fickle? When I make my plans, do I make them from selfish motives, ready to say "Yes, yes" and "No, no" at the same time? [18] As God is true, my promise to you was not a "Yes" and a "No." [19] For Jesus Christ, the Son of God, who was preached among you by Silas, Timothy, and myself, is not one who is "Yes" and "No." On the contrary, he is God's "Yes"; [20] for it is he who is the "Yes" to all of God's promises. This is the reason that through Jesus Christ our "Amen" is said, to the glory of God. [21] For it is God himself who makes us sure, with you, of our life in Christ; it is God himself who has set us apart, [22] who placed his mark of ownership upon us, and who gave the Holy Spirit in our hearts as the guarantee of all that he has for us.

[23] I call upon God as my witness — he knows my heart! It was in order to spare you that I decided not to go to Corinth. [24] We are not trying to dictate to you what you must believe, for you stand firm in the faith. Instead, we are working with you for your own happiness.

2 So I made up my mind about this: I would not come to you again to make you sad. [2] For if I were to make you sad, who would be left to cheer me up? Only the very persons I had saddened! [3] That is why I wrote that letter to you — I did not want to come to you and be made sad

by the very people who should make me glad. For I am convinced that when I am happy, then you too are happy. ⁴ I wrote you with a greatly troubled and distressed heart, and with many tears, not to make you sad, but to make you realize how much I love you all.

Forgiveness for the Offender

⁵ Now, if anyone has made somebody sad, he has not done it to me but to you; or to some of you, at least, since I do not want to be too hard on you. ⁶ It is enough for this person that he has been punished in this way by most of you. ⁷ Now, however, you should forgive him and encourage him, to keep him from becoming so sad as to give up completely. ⁸ Let him know, then, I beg you, that you really do love him. ⁹ For this is the reason I wrote you that letter: I wanted to find out how well you had stood the test, and whether you are always ready to obey my instructions. ¹⁰ When you forgive someone for what he has done, I forgive him too. For when I forgive — if, indeed, I have forgiven any wrong — I do it because of you, in Christ's presence, ¹¹ in order to keep Satan from getting the upper hand over us; for we know what his plans are.

Paul's Anxiety in Troas

¹² When I arrived in Troas to preach the Good News about Christ, I found that the Lord had opened the way for the work there. ¹³ But I was deeply worried because I could not find our brother Titus. So I said good-bye to the people there, and went on to Macedonia.

Victory through Christ

¹⁴ But thanks be to God! For in union with Christ we are always led by God as prisoners in Christ's victory procession. Like a sweet smell that spreads everywhere, God uses us to make Christ known to all men. ¹⁵ For we are like the sweet smell of the incense that Christ burns to God which goes out to those who are being saved and to those who are being lost. ¹⁶ For those who are being lost, it is a deadly stench that kills; for those who are being saved, it is a fragrance that brings life. Who, then, is capable for such a task? ¹⁷ We are not like so many others, who handle God's message as if it were cheap merchandise;

but because God has sent us, we speak with sincerity in his presence, as servants of Christ.

Servants of the New Covenant

3 Does this sound as if we were again boasting about ourselves? Could it be that, like some other people, we need letters of recommendation to you or from you? [2] You yourselves are the letter we have, written on our hearts, for everyone to know and read. [3] It is clear that Christ himself wrote this letter and sent it by us. It is written not with ink on stone tablets, but on human hearts, with the Spirit of the living God.

[4] We say this because we have confidence in God through Christ. [5] For there is nothing in us that allows us to claim that we are capable of doing this work. The capacity we have comes from God: [6] for it is he who made us capable of serving the new covenant, which consists not

of a written law, but of the Spirit. The written law brings death, but the Spirit gives life.

[7] The Law was carved in letters on stone tablets, and God's glory appeared when it was given. Even though it faded away, the brightness on Moses' face was so strong that the people of Israel could not keep their eyes fixed on him. If the Law, whose service was to bring death, came with such glory, [8] how much greater is the glory that belongs to the service of the Spirit! [9] The service by which men are condemned was glorious; how much more glorious is the service by which men are declared innocent! [10] We may say that, because of the far brighter glory now, the glory that was so bright in the past is gone. [11] For if

there was glory in that which lasted for a while, how much more glory is there in that which lasts for ever!

¹² Because we have this hope, we are very bold. ¹³ We are not like Moses, who had to put a veil over his face, so that the people of Israel might not see the brightness fade and disappear. ¹⁴ Their minds, indeed, were closed; and to this very day their minds are covered with the same veil, as they read the books of the old covenant. The veil is removed only when a man is joined to Christ. ¹⁵ Even today, whenever they read the Law of Moses, the veil still covers their minds. ¹⁶ But it is removed, as the scripture says: "Moses' veil was removed when he turned to the Lord." ¹⁷ Now, "the Lord" in this passage is the Spirit; and where the Spirit of the Lord is present, there is freedom. ¹⁸ All of us, then, reflect the glory of the Lord with uncovered faces; and that same glory, coming from the Lord who is the Spirit, transforms us into his very likeness, in an ever greater degree of glory.

Spiritual Treasure in Clay Pots

4 God, in his mercy, has given us this service, and so we do not become discouraged. ² We put aside all secret and shameful deeds; we do not act with deceit, nor do we falsify the word of God. In the full light of truth, we live in God's sight and try to commend ourselves to everyone's good conscience. ³ For if the gospel we preach is hidden, it is hidden only to those who are being lost. ⁴ They do not believe because their minds have been kept in the dark by the evil god of this world. He keeps them from seeing the light shining on them, the light that comes from the Good News about the glory of Christ, who is the exact likeness of God. ⁵ For it is not ourselves that we preach: we preach Jesus Christ as Lord, and ourselves as your servants for Jesus' sake. ⁶ The God who said, "Out of darkness the light shall shine!" is the same God who made his light shine in our hearts, to bring us the light of the knowledge of God's glory, shining in the face of Christ.

⁷ Yet we who have this spiritual treasure are like common clay pots, to show that the supreme power belongs to God, not to us. ⁸ We are often troubled, but not crushed; sometimes in doubt, but never in despair; ⁹ there are many enemies, but we are never without a friend; and though badly hurt at times, we are not destroyed. ¹⁰ At all

times we carry in our mortal bodies the death of Jesus, so that his life also may be seen in our bodies. ¹¹ Throughout our lives we are always in danger of death for Jesus' sake, in order that his life may be seen in this mortal body of ours. ¹² This means that death is at work in us; but life is at work in you.

¹³ The scripture says, "I spoke because I believed." In the same spirit of faith, we also speak because we believe. ¹⁴ For we know that God, who raised the Lord Jesus to life, will also raise us up with Jesus and bring us, together with you, into his presence. ¹⁵ All this is for your sake; and as God's grace reaches more and more people, they will offer more prayers of thanksgiving, to the glory of God.

Living by Faith

¹⁶ For this reason we never become discouraged. Even though our physical being is gradually decaying, yet our spiritual being is renewed day after day. ¹⁷ And this small and temporary trouble we suffer will bring us a tremendous and eternal glory, much greater than the trouble. ¹⁸ For we fix our attention, not on things that are seen, but on things that are unseen. What can be seen lasts only for a time; but what cannot be seen lasts for ever.

5 For we know that when this tent we live in — our body here on earth — is torn down, God will have a house in heaven for us to live in, a home he himself made, which will last for ever. ² And now we sigh, so great is our desire to have our home which is in heaven put on over us; ³ for by being clothed with it we shall not be found without a body. ⁴ While we live in this earthly tent we groan with a feeling of oppression; it is not that we want to get rid of our earthly body, but that we want to have the heavenly one put on over us, so that what is mortal will be swallowed up by life. ⁵ God is the one who has prepared us for this change, and he gave us his Spirit as the guarantee of all that he has for us.

⁶ So we are always full of courage. We know that as long as we are at home in this body we are away from the Lord's home. ⁷ For our life is a matter of faith, not of sight. ⁸ We are full of courage, and would much prefer to leave our home in this body and be at home with the Lord. ⁹ More than anything else, however, we want to

please him, whether in our home here or there. [10] For all of us must appear before Christ, to be judged by him, so that each one may receive what he deserves, according to what he has done, good or bad, in his bodily life.

Friendship with God through Christ

[11] We know what it means to fear the Lord, and so we try to persuade men. God knows us completely, and I hope that in your hearts you know me as well. [12] We are not trying to recommend ourselves to you again; rather, we are trying to give you a good reason to be proud of us, so that you will be able to answer those who boast about a man's appearance, and not about his character. [13] Are we really insane? It is for God's sake. Or are we sane? It is for your sake. [14] For we are ruled by Christ's love for us, now that we recognize that one man died for all men, which means that all men take part in his death. [15] He died for all men so that those who live should no longer live for themselves, but only for him who died and was raised to life for their sake.

[16] No longer, then, do we judge anyone by human standards. Even if at one time we judged Christ according to human standards, we no longer do so. [17] When anyone is joined to Christ he is a new being: the old is gone, the new has come. [18] All this is done by God, who through Christ changed us from enemies into his friends, and gave us the task of making others his friends also. [19] Our message is that God was making friends of all men through Christ. God did not keep an account of their sins against them, and he has given us the message of how he makes them his friends.

[20] Here we are, then, speaking for Christ, as though God himself were appealing to you through us: on Christ's behalf, we beg you, let God change you from enemies into friends! [21] Chris' was without sin, but God made him share our sin in order that we, in union with him, might share the righteousness of God.

6 In our work together with God, then, we beg of you: you have received God's grace, and you must not let it be wasted. [2] Hear what God says:

"I heard you in the hour of my favour,
I helped you in the day of salvation."

Listen! This is the hour to receive God's favour, today is

the day to be saved!

⁸ We do not want anyone to find fault with our work, so we try not to put obstacles in anyone's way. ⁴ Instead, in everything we do we show that we are God's servants, by enduring troubles, hardships, and difficulties with great patience. ⁵ We have been beaten, jailed, and mobbed; we have been overworked and have gone without sleep or food. ⁶ By our purity, knowledge, patience, and kindness we have shown ourselves to be God's servants; by the Holy Spirit, by our true love, ⁷ by our message of truth, and by the power of God. We have righteousness as our weapon, both to attack and to defend ourselves. ⁸ We are honoured and disgraced; we are insulted and praised. We are treated as liars, yet we speak the truth; ⁹ as unknown, yet we are known by all; as though we were dead, but, as you see, we live on. Although punished, we are not killed; ¹⁰ although saddened, we are always glad; we seem poor, but we make many people rich; we seem to have nothing, yet we really possess everything.

¹¹ Dear friends in Corinth! We have spoken frankly to you, we have opened wide our hearts. ¹² We have not closed our hearts to you; it is you who have closed your hearts to us. ¹³ I speak now as though you were my children: show us the same feelings that we have for you. Open wide your hearts!

Warning against Pagan Influences

¹⁴ Do not try to work together as equals with unbe-

lievers, for it cannot be done. How can right and wrong be partners? How can light and darkness live together? ¹⁵ How can Christ and the Devil agree? What does a believer have in common with an unbeliever? ¹⁶ How can God's temple come to terms with pagan idols? For we are the temple of the living God! As God himself has said:

> "I will make my home with them and live
> among them,
> I will be their God, and they shall be my
> people."

¹⁷ And so the Lord says:

> "You must leave them, and separate your-
> selves from them.
> Have nothing to do with what is unclean,
> And I will accept you.
> ¹⁸ I will be your father,
> And you shall be my sons and daughters,
> Says the Lord Almighty."

7 All these promises are made to us, my dear friends! Let us, therefore, purify ourselves from everything that makes body or soul unclean, and let us seek to be completely holy, by living in the fear of God.

Paul's Joy

² Make room for us in your hearts. We have done wrong to no one, we have ruined no one, nor tried to take advantage of anyone. ³ I do not say this to condemn you; for, as I have said before, you are so dear to us that we are together always, whether we live or die. ⁴ I am so sure of

you, I take such pride in you! In all our troubles I am still full of courage, I am running over with joy.

⁵ Even after we arrived in Macedonia we did not have any rest. There were troubles everywhere, quarrels with others, fears in our hearts. ⁶ But God, who encourages the downhearted, encouraged us with the coming of Titus. ⁷ It was not only his coming, but also his report of how you encouraged him. He told us how much you want to see me, how sorry you are, how ready you are to defend me; and so I am even happier now.

⁸ For even if that letter of mine made you sad, I am not sorry I wrote it. I could have been sorry about it when I saw that the letter made you sad for a while. ⁹ But now I am happy — not because I made you sad, but because your sadness made you change your ways. That sadness was used by God, and so we caused you no harm. ¹⁰ For the sadness that is used by God brings a change of heart that leads to salvation — and there is no regret in that! But worldly sadness causes death. ¹¹ See what God did with this sadness of yours: how earnest it has made you, how eager to prove your innocence! Such indignation, such alarm, such feelings, such devotion, such readiness to punish wrongdoing! You have shown yourselves to be without fault in the whole matter.

¹² So, even though I wrote that letter, I did it, not because of the one who did wrong, or the one who was wronged. Instead, I wrote it to make plain to you, in God's sight, how deep is your devotion to us. ¹³ That is why we were encouraged.

Not only were we encouraged; how happy Titus made us with his happiness over the way in which all of you helped to cheer him up. ¹⁴ I did boast of you to him, and you have not disappointed me. We have always spoken the truth to you. In the same way, the boast we made to Titus has proved true. ¹⁵ And so his love for you grows stronger, as he remembers how all of you were ready to obey, how you welcomed him with fear and trembling. ¹⁶ How happy I am that I can depend on you completely!

Christian Giving

8 We want you to know, brothers, what God's grace has done in the churches in Macedonia. ² They have been severely tested by the troubles they went through; but

their joy was so great that they were extremely generous in their giving, even though they were very poor. ⁸ I assure you, they gave as much as they were able, and even more than that; of their own free will ⁴ they begged us and insisted on the privilege of having a part in helping God's people in Judea. ⁵ It was more than we could have hoped for! First they gave themselves to the Lord; and then, by God's will, they gave themselves to us as well. ⁶ So we urged Titus, who began this work, to continue it and help you complete this special service of love. ⁷ You are so rich in all you have: in faith, speech, and knowledge, in your eagerness to help, and in your love for us. And so we want you to be generous also in this service of love.

⁸ I am not laying down any rules. But by showing how eager others are to help, I am trying to find out how real your own love is. ⁹ For you know the grace of our Lord Jesus Christ: rich as he was, he made himself poor for your sake, in order to make you rich by means of his poverty.

¹⁰ This is my opinion on the matter: it is better for you to finish now what you began last year. You were the first, not only to act, but also to be willing to act. ¹¹ On with it, then, and finish the job! Be as eager to finish it as you were to plan it, and do it with what you have. ¹² For if you are eager to give, God will accept your gift on the basis of what you have to give, not on what you don't have.

¹³⁻¹⁴ I am not trying to relieve others by putting a burden on you; but since you have plenty at this time, it is only fair that you should help those who are in need. Then, when you are in need and they have plenty, they will help you. In this way both are treated equally. ¹⁵ As the scripture says,

"The man who gathered much
Did not have too much,
And the man who gathered little
Did not have too little."

¹⁶ How we thank God for making Titus as eager as we are to help you! ¹⁷ Not only did he welcome our request; he was so eager to help that of his own free will he decided to go to you. ¹⁸ With him we are sending the brother who is highly respected in all the churches for his work in preaching the gospel. ¹⁹ And besides that, he has been

chosen and appointed by the churches to travel with us as
we carry out this service of love for the Lord's glory, and
to show that we want to help.

²⁰ We are being careful not to stir up any complaints
about the way we handle this generous gift. ²¹ Our purpose is to do what is right, not only in the sight of the
Lord, but also in the sight of men.

²² So we are sending our brother with them; we have
tested him many times, and found him always very eager
to help. And now that he has so much confidence in you,
he is all the more eager to help. ²³ As for Titus, he is my
partner who works with me to help you; as for the other
brothers who are going with him, they represent the
churches and bring glory to Christ. ²⁴ Show your love to
them, that all the churches will be sure of it and know
that we are right in boasting of you.

Help for Fellow Christians

9 There is really no need for me to write you about the
help being sent to God's people in Judea. ² I know that
you are willing to help, and I have boasted of you to the
people in Macedonia. "The brothers in Greece," I said,
"have been ready to help since last year." Your eagerness
has stirred up most of them. ³ Now I am sending these
brothers, so that our boasting of you in this matter may
not turn out to be empty words; but, just as I said, you will
be ready with your help. ⁴ Or else, if the people from
Macedonia should come with me and find out that you are
not ready, how ashamed we would be — not to speak of
your shame — for feeling so sure of you! ⁵ So I thought
it necessary to urge these brothers to go to you ahead of
me and get ready in advance the gift you promised to
make. Then it will be ready when I arrive, and it will
show that you give because you want to, not because you
have to.

⁶ Remember this: the man who plants few seeds will
have a small crop; the one who plants many seeds will
have a large crop. ⁷ Each one should give, then, as he has
decided, not with regret or out of a sense of duty; for God
loves the one who gives gladly. ⁸ And God is able to give
you more than you need, so that you will always have all
you need for yourselves and more than enough for every
good cause. ⁹ As the scripture says,

"He gives generously to the poor,
His kindness lasts for ever."

20 And God, who supplies seed for the sower and bread to eat, will also supply you with all the seed you need and make it grow, to produce a rich harvest from your generosity. 11 He will always make you rich enough to be generous at all times, so that many will thank God for your gifts through us. 12 For this service you perform not only meets the needs of God's people, but also produces an outpouring of grateful thanks to God. 13 And because of the proof which this service of yours brings, many will give glory to God for your loyalty to the gospel of Christ, which you profess, and for your generosity in sharing with them and all others. 14 And so they will pray for you with great affection for you because of the extraordinary grace God has shown you. 15 Let us thank God for his priceless gift!

Paul Defends His Ministry

10 I, Paul, make a personal appeal to you — I who am said to be meek and mild when I am with you, but bold towards you when I am away from you. I beg of you, by the gentleness and kindness of Christ: 2 Do not force me to be bold with you when I come; for I am sure I can be bold with those who say that we act from worldly motives. 3 It is true that we live in the world; but we do not fight from worldly motives. 4 The weapons we use in our fight are not the world's weapons, but God's powerful weapons, with which to destroy strongholds. We destroy false arguments; 5 we pull down every proud obstacle that is raised against the knowledge of God; we take every thought captive and make it obey Christ. 6 And after you have proved your complete loyalty, we will be ready to punish any act of disloyalty.

7 You are looking at things as they are on the outside. Is there someone there who reckons himself to be Christ's man? Well, let him think again about himself, for we are Christ's men just as much as he is. 8 For I am not ashamed, even if I have boasted somewhat too much of the authority that the Lord has given us — authority to build you up, that is, not to tear you down. 9 I do not want it to appear that I am trying to frighten you with my letters. 10 Someone will say, "Paul's letters are severe and

strong, but when he is with us in person he is weak, and his words are nothing!" ¹¹ Such a person must understand that there is no difference between what we write in our letters when we are away, and what we will do when we are there with you.

¹² Of course we would not dare classify ourselves or compare ourselves with some of those who rate themselves so highly. How stupid they are! They make up their own standards to measure themselves by, and judge themselves by their own standards! ¹³ As for us, however, our boasting will not go beyond certain limits; it will stay within the limits of the work which God has set for us, which includes our work among you. ¹⁴ And since you are within those

limits, we did not go beyond them when we came to you, bringing the Good News about Christ. ¹⁵ So we do not boast of the work that others have done beyond the limits God set for us. Instead, we hope that your faith may grow, and that we may be able to do a much greater work among you, always within the limits that God has set. ¹⁶ Then we can preach the Good News in other countries beyond you, and shall not have to boast of work already done in another man's field.

¹⁷ But as the scripture says, "Whoever wants to boast, must boast of what the Lord has done." ¹⁸ Because a man is really approved when the Lord thinks well of him, not when he thinks well of himself.

Paul and the False Apostles

11 I wish you would tolerate me, even when I am a bit foolish. Please do! [2] I am jealous for you just as God is; for you are like a pure virgin whom I have promised in marriage to one man only, who is Christ. [3] I am afraid that your minds will be corrupted and that you will abandon your full and pure devotion to Christ — in the same way that Eve was deceived by the snake's clever lies. [4] For you gladly tolerate anyone who comes to you and preaches a different Jesus, not the one we preached; and you accept a spirit and a gospel completely different from the Spirit and the gospel you received from us!

[5] I do not think that I am the least bit inferior to those very special "apostles" of yours! [6] Perhaps I am an amateur in speaking, but certainly not in knowledge; we have made this clear to you at all times and in all conditions.

[7] I did not charge you a thing when I preached the Good News of God to you; I humbled myself in order to make you great. Was that wrong of me? [8] While I was working among you I was paid by other churches. I was robbing them, so to speak, to help you. [9] And during the time I was with you I did not bother you for help when I needed money; for the brothers who came from Macedonia brought me everything I needed. As in the past, so in the future: I will never be a burden to you! [10] By Christ's truth in me, I promise that this boast of mine will not be silenced anywhere in all of Greece. [11] Why do I say this? Because I don't love you? God knows I do!

¹² I will go on doing what I am doing now, in order to keep those other "apostles" from having any reason for boasting and saying that they work in the same way that we do. ¹³ Those men are not true apostles — they are false apostles, who lie about their work and change themselves to look like real apostles of Christ. ¹⁴ Well, no wonder! Even Satan can change himself to look like an angel of light! ¹⁵ So it is no great thing if his servants change themselves to look like servants of right. In the end they will get exactly what they deserve for the things they do.

Paul's Sufferings as an Apostle

¹⁶ I repeat: no one should think that I am a fool. But if you do, at least accept me as a fool, just so I will have a little to boast of. ¹⁷ Of course what I am saying now is not what the Lord would have me say; in this matter of boasting I am really talking like a fool. ¹⁸ But since there are so many who boast for merely human reasons, I will do the same. ¹⁹ You yourselves are so wise, and so you gladly tolerate fools! ²⁰ You will tolerate anyone who orders you around, or takes advantage of you, or traps you, or looks down on you, or slaps you in the face. ²¹ I am ashamed to admit it: we were too timid to do that!

But if anyone dares to boast of something — I am talking like a fool — I will be just as daring. ²² Are they Hebrews? So am I. Are they Israelites? So am I. Are they Abraham's descendants? So am I. ²³ Are they Christ's servants? I sound like a madman — but I am a better servant than they are! I have worked much harder, I have been in prison more times, I have been whipped much more, and I have been near death more often. ²⁴ Five times I was given the thirty-nine lashes by the Jews; ²⁵ three times I was whipped by the Romans, and once I was stoned; I have been in three shipwrecks, and once I spent twenty-four hours in the water. ²⁶ In my many travels I have been in danger from floods and from robbers, in danger from fellow Jews and from Gentiles; there have been dangers in the cities, dangers in the wilds, dangers on the high seas, and dangers from false friends. ²⁷ There has been work and toil; often I have gone without sleep; I have been hungry and thirsty; I have often been without enough food, shelter, or clothing. ²⁸ And, not to mention other things, every day I am under the pressure of my concern for all the churches. ²⁹ When someone is weak, then I feel weak too; when someone falls into sin, I am filled with distress.

³⁰ If I must boast, I will boast of things that show how weak I am. ³¹ The God and Father of the Lord Jesus — blessed be his name for ever! — knows that I am not lying. ³² When I was in Damascus, the governor under King Aretas placed guards at the city gates to arrest me. ³³ But I was let down in a basket, through an opening in the wall, and escaped from him.

Paul's Visions and Revelations

12 I have to boast, even though it doesn't do any good. But I will now talk about visions and revelations given me by the Lord. ² I know a certain Christian man who fourteen years ago was snatched up to the highest heaven (I do not know whether this actually happened, or whether he had a vision — only God knows). ³ I repeat, I know that this man was snatched to Paradise (again, I do not know whether this actually happened, or whether it was a vision — only God knows), ⁴ and there he heard things which cannot be put into words, things that human lips may not speak. ⁵ So I will boast of this man — but I will not boast about myself, except the things that show how weak I am. ⁶ If I wanted to boast, I would not be a fool, because I would be telling the truth. But I will not boast, because I do not want anyone to have a higher opinion of me than he has from what he has seen me do and heard me say.

⁷ But to keep me from being puffed up with pride because of the wonderful things I saw, I was given a painful physical ailment, which acts as Satan's messenger to beat me and keep me from being proud. ⁸ Three times I prayed to the Lord about this, and asked him to take it away. ⁹ His answer was, "My grace is all you need; for my power is strongest when you are weak." I am most happy, then, to be proud of my weaknesses, in order to feel the protection of Christ's power over me. ¹⁰ I am content with weaknesses, insults, hardships, persecutions, and difficulties for Christ's sake. For when I am weak, then I am strong.

Paul's Concern for the Corinthians

¹¹ I am acting like a fool — but you have made me do it. You are the ones who ought to show your approval of me. For even if I am nothing, I am in no way inferior to those very special "apostles" of yours. ¹² The things that prove that I am an apostle were done with all patience among you; there were signs and wonders and miracles. ¹³ How were you treated any worse than the other churches, except that I did not bother you for help? Please forgive me for being so unfair!

¹⁴ This is now the third time that I am ready to come to visit you — and I will not make any demands on you. It is you I want, not your money. After all, children should not have to provide for their parents, but parents should provide for their children. ¹⁵ I will be glad to spend all I have, and myself as well, in order to help you. Will you love me less because I love you so much?

¹⁶ You will agree, then, that I was not a burden to you. But, someone will say, I was tricky and trapped you with lies. ¹⁷ How? Did I take advantage of you through any of the messengers I sent? ¹⁸ I begged Titus to go, and I sent the other Christian brother with him. Would you say that Titus took advantage of you? Do not he and I act from the very same motives and behave in the same way?

¹⁹ Perhaps you think that all along we have been trying to defend ourselves before you. No! We speak as Christ would have us speak, in the presence of God, and everything we do, dear friends, is done to help you. ²⁰ I am afraid that when I get there I will find you different from what I would like you to be and you will find me different from what you would like me to be. I am afraid that I will find quarrelling and jealousy, hot tempers and selfishness, insults and gossip, pride and disorder. ²¹ I am afraid that the next time I come my God will humiliate me in your presence, and I shall weep over many who sinned in the past and have not repented of the immoral things they have done, their sexual sins and lustful deeds.

Final Warnings and Greetings

13 This is now the third time that I am coming to visit you. "Any accusation must be upheld by the evidence of two or three witnesses" — as the scripture

says. [2] I want to tell you who have sinned in the past, and all the others; I said it before, during my second visit to you, but I will say it again now that I am away: the next time I come nobody will escape punishment. [3] You will have all the proof you want that Christ speaks through me. When he deals with you he is not weak; instead he shows his power among you. [4] For even though it was in weakness that he was put to death on the cross, it is by God's power that he lives. In union with him we also are weak; but in our relations with you, we shall live with him by God's power.

[5] Put yourselves to the test and judge yourselves, to find out whether you are living in faith. Surely you know that Christ Jesus is in you? — unless you have completely failed. [6] I trust you will know that we are not failures. [7] We pray to God that you will do no wrong — not in order to show that we are a success, but that you may do what is right, even though we may seem to be failures. [8] For we cannot do a thing against God's truth, but only for it. [9] We are glad when we are weak but you are strong. And so we also pray that you will become perfect. [10] That is why I write this while I am away from you; it is so that when I arrive I will not have to deal harshly with you in using the authority that the Lord gave me — authority to build you up, not to tear you down.

[11] And now, brothers, good-bye! Strive for perfection; listen to what I say; agree with one another, and live in peace. And the God of love and peace will be with you.

[12] Greet one another with a brotherly kiss.

All God's people send you their greetings.

[13] The grace of the Lord Jesus Christ, the love of God, and the fellowship of the Holy Spirit be with you all.

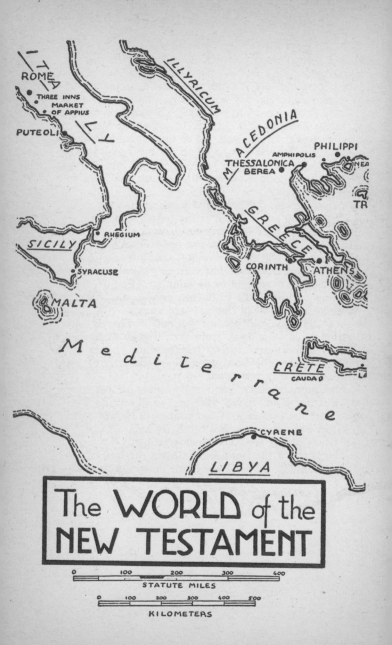

The WORLD of the NEW TESTAMENT

THE BIBLE READING FELLOWSHIP

Readers of this commentary may wish to follow a regular pattern of Bible reading, designed to cover the Bible roughly on the basis of a book a month. Suitable Notes (send for details) with helpful exposition and prayers are provided by the Bible Reading Fellowship three times a year (January to April, May to August, September to December), and are available from:—

UK   The Bible Reading Fellowship,
St Michael's House,
2 Elizabeth Street,
London SW1.W 9RQ.

USA   The Bible Reading Fellowship,
P.O. Box 299, Winter Park,
Florida 32789,
USA.

AUSTRALIA The Bible Reading Fellowship,
Jamieson House,
Constitution Avenue,
Reid,
Canberra, ACT 2601,
Australia.

Also available in Fount Paperbacks

A Historical Introduction to the New Testament
ROBERT GRANT

'This splendid book is a New Testament introduction with a difference . . . All students of the New Testament will welcome this original and courageous study.'
Professor James S. Stewart

The Historical Geography of the Holy Land
G. ADAM SMITH

'A classic which has fascinated and instructed generations of students. This masterpiece among the vast literature on the Bible . . . will continue to delight readers as well as to inform.'
H. H. Rowley

The Dead Sea Scrolls 1947-1969
EDMUND WILSON

'A lucid narrative of the discovery of the scrolls which soon turns into a learned detective story; then an account of the excitement, the consternation and the intrigues.'
V. S. Pritchett, New Statesman

The Gospels and the Jesus of History
XAVIER LEON-DUFOUR

'This book is far more than an introduction to the study of the Gospels. With its detailed study of the Gospels and of the other New Testament books it is an excellent introduction to the Christology of the New Testament.' *William Barclay*

Also available in Fount Paperbacks

Prayer for the Day
WILF WILKINSON

A new collection of talks by one of the most popular religious broadcasters in Britain. Mr Wilkinson's introduction is entitled 'The Prayers of an Ordinary Man' and that is what they are – they come out of ordinary experiences, they face ordinary difficulties.

The True Wilderness
H. A. WILLIAMS

'I was moved by the plainness and lucidity of *The True Wilderness*. Mr Williams reminds us simply and eloquently of charity and the way in which "our intrinsic tenderness has been violated".'

John Osborne, The Observer

Into the New Age
STEPHEN VERNEY

This book is a declaration that now is the springtime of the Christian Church. As the human race faces the choice between catastrophe and an evolutionary leap forward in the realm of the spirit, Christianity is being profoundly renewed.

The Life of Jesus Christ
LORD LONGFORD

'It is an impressive piece of work and will help many. It will do much good, and as a devotional commentary on the life of Jesus it is excellent and will bear reading and re-reading. Many people will be glad Lord Longford wrote this book. It is a book of faith written by a man of faith.'

Bishop Nicholas Allenby, Daily Telegraph